French crime fiction
and the Second World War

MANCHESTER
1824

Manchester University Press

Cultural History of Modern War
Series editors

Ana Carden-Coyne, Peter Gatrell, Max Jones, Penny Summerfield and
Bertrand Taithe

Already published

Centre for the
Cultural History
of War

French crime fiction and the Second World War

Past crimes, present memories

~

CLAIRE GORRARA

Manchester University Press
Manchester and New York
distributed exclusively in the USA by Palgrave

Published by Manchester University Press
Oxford Road, Manchester M13 9NR, UK
and Room 400, 175 Fifth Avenue, New York, NY 10010, USA
www.manchesteruniversitypress.co.uk

Distributed in the United States exclusively by
Palgrave Macmillan, 175 Fifth Avenue, New York,
NY 10010, USA

Distributed in Canada exclusively by
UBC Press, University of British Columbia, 2029 West Mall,
Vancouver, BC, Canada V6T 1Z2

British Library Cataloguing-in-Publication Data
A catalogue record for this book is available from the British Library
Library of Congress Cataloging-in-Publication Data applied for

ISBN 978 0 7190 8265 8 *hardback*

First published 2012

Edited and typeset
by Frances Hackeson Freelance Publishing Services, Brinscall, Lancs
Printed in Great Britain
by MPG Books Group, UK

Contents

Preface and acknowledgements

This book would not have been possible without help from a number of sources. Firstly, I would like to thank the School of European Studies, Cardiff University, for granting me a period of research leave in which to complete this monograph in 2011. Particular thanks are due to colleagues within the French department who covered my absence. This monograph also benefited from two research trips to Paris in 2007 supported by the British Academy and I gratefully acknowledge the Academy's support. The final stages of research for this project were enriched by a short period as a Visiting Fellow of the Centre for Cultural Memory at the Institute of Germanic and Romance Studies, University of London, in 2011. I would like to thank Naomi Segal and Katia Pizzi for their warm welcome.

Earlier versions of two chapters of the book have already appeared in print. A revised version of Chapter 1 was published as 'Conflicted masculinities: figures of resistance in French crime fiction', in Katharina Hall and Kathryn N. Jones (eds), *Constructions of Conflict: Transmitting Memories of the Past in European Historiography, Culture and Media* (Bern: Peter Lang, 2011), pp. 91–110. A version of Chapter 2 was published in the *South Central Review*, 27:1–2 (2010), 3–20, a Johns Hopkins University Press publication. Permission to reprint is gratefully acknowledged. Throughout, all translations from the French original are my own unless otherwise specified.

I would also like to thank colleagues and friends who have helped in the writing of this book, especially Hanna Diamond who read through a draft version of the manuscript and Rachael Langford who provided insightful comments on the Introduction and Conclusion. It is also a great pleasure to thank friends and colleagues who have contributed with encouragement and support at various stages in the project: Margaret

Atack, Béatrice Blanchet, Richard Golsan, Katharina Hall, Leah D. Hewitt, Kathryn N. Jones, Ruth Kitchen, Christopher Lloyd, Kevin Passmore, Solange Pierrat-Dané, David Platten, Heather Worthington and colleagues of the Crime Narratives in Context research network at Cardiff University. Thanks must also go to my mother, Jackie Gorrara, an avid crime fiction reader and my unofficial researcher for all things crime related, and my parents-in-law, Martin and Mariette Boyle, for their support and hospitality at Rushgill.

Lastly, this book is dedicated to my husband, Joe Boyle, and children, Jacob and Edith, with all my love.

Introduction

Mapping French memories of the Second World War

La valise la plus lourde dans les voyages est celle, invisible, qui renferme des souvenirs.[1]

From heroic war narratives of resistance to the collusions and compromises of collaboration and the human tragedy of wartime anti-Semitism, deportation and extermination, memories of the Second World War continue to resonate in French public consciousness. Even with the passage of time and the gradual disappearance of those who experienced events, the Second World War remains a 'disunited memory', one which divides as much as unites communities of remembrance in contemporary France.[2] This study aims to examine the memorial legacies of the Second World War in a cultural arena which has been little studied: crime fiction. For, as this study will contend, crime fiction, as a form of popular culture, constructs narratives of war that exploit connections between war and crime, guilt and responsibility, justice and resolution, all couplings that have marked collective understandings of the war years in France. Historically contingent and highly variable, these popular formulations offer a different perspective on the evolution of French war memories compared to other more public and political narratives. They open up new avenues for investigation that chart the two-way traffic between official discourses of war and popular reconstructions. For while many French crime novels incorporate and adapt war stories prevalent at the point of their composition, others engage in polemical struggle with dominant narratives, offering counter-histories of defeat, occupation and liberation. In contributing to popular culture's shaping of war memory, French crime fiction provides a colourful corpus of texts with which to extend analysis of what it means to live in the shadow of such a past.

~1~

This introduction will set out the conceptual, historical and literary-critical foundations on which this study is built. It will begin by mapping memory, exploring some of the major approaches to the study of collective memory. It will focus in particular on cultural memory and the significance of fictional forms as some of the most protean and influential media of memory. It will then examine the fraught historical legacies of the Second World War, with an emphasis on France. It will engage with Henry Rousso's pioneering model of the evolution of French memories of the Second World War, the Vichy syndrome, and assess its applicability for fictional representations of the Second World War in France. Finally, this introduction will consider approaches to the study of popular culture and investigate the narrative template of crime fiction, above all its generic engagement with cultural memories of the Second World War. The introduction will conclude with a discussion of the parameters and working methodologies of the study and a brief overview of the chapter organisation and the major themes and debates.

Mapping memory

Memory studies have always operated at the intersection of a number of disciplinary fields. From history and cultural studies to neuroscience and cognitive psychology, researchers have asked questions concerning the role of memory in shaping not only our relationship to the past but also our sense of ourselves in the present and the 'advancing stories' we tell of ourselves and our culture into the future.[3] Indeed, memory's role in framing present-day and future relations has led to studies of the ethics of memory, and how the principles and values attributed to memory might be invoked in processes of political and social reconciliation,[4] as well as the politics of memory, and the potential of national memories to mould political cultures, above all at times of crisis and war.[5] Memory studies have also been sensitive to issues of amnesia and forgetting. Psychoanalysis and trauma theory have expanded the scope of memory studies to incorporate discussions of the representability of the past, particularly the Holocaust, and the ways in which the witness or survivor grapples with the need to tell but the impossibility of telling.[6]

Culturally informed perspectives on memory converge on two key observations: firstly, that memory is an act or process of recollection in the present. Memory is 'a term which directs our attention not to the past but to *the past-present relation*. It is because "the past" has this living active existence in the present that it matters so much politically'.[7] In this conceptualisation of memory, memory is not a virtual storehouse of past events awaiting recuperation which can be restored into the present, whole and true. Instead, the emphasis is upon 'the idea that memories of a shared past are collectively constructed and reconstructed in the present rather than resurrected from the past',[8] and that they are informed by historically and culturally specific processes which determine which versions of past events gain currency at which time and who or what is entitled to speak about the past in the present. Secondly, many cultural critics of memory stress memory's strategic or political impact on the present. For cultural historians such as Katherine Hodgkin and Susannah Radstone, memory revolves around questions of power, authority and control: 'Memory is political: it remains a site of struggle over meaning.'[9] What is remembered, and how, is inevitably shaped by contemporary social and political relations and cannot escape its inflection by the demands of dominant groups who have the power to promote or silence particular versions of the past. However, this recurrent imagery of struggle and contestation in memory studies should not be interpreted as a sign that repressive authority is always at work in the formulation of memories or that memory should be reduced to politics or political use. Multiple memories in the public arena can be representative of productive exchange and can foster social cohesion. Indeed, the ways in which we represent a shared past, our 'memory discourses', influence our identity as individuals, as well as how we relate to broader social groupings.[10] The complexities of the relationships between memory, identity and culture have informed the work of some of the most significant cultural theorists of memory.

Studies of collective memory, above all, demonstrate how scholars have been preoccupied with the diverse and often elusive ways in which individual memory is translated into larger groupings and how such memory constructs become embedded in social structures. Much of this work is indebted to the insights of French sociologist Maurice Halbwachs and his model of collective memory. This model posits the notion that 'no memory is possible outside frameworks used by people living in society to determine and retrieve their recollections'.[11] For Halbwachs, all memory is situated within social frameworks which provide the individual with the interpretative tools and cultural context to make sense of her or his personal memories. These memories are necessarily reshaped over time as the individual's perceptions of her or his past alters in response to the pressures of society and her or his life experiences. For, in Halbwachs's model of collective memory, modern societies are perceived to 'penetrate and insinuate themselves more deeply into their members because of the multiplicity and complexity of relations of all kinds with which they envelop their members'.[12] Even when the individual believes her or himself to be most fully alone, she or he remains a resolutely social being bound into a range of collective identities.[13]

Halbwachs's study of collective memory within modern society has been developed in the work of subsequent theorists, such as Jan Assmann who has reworked the discussion of group memories transmitted across generations. Assmann creates a temporal framing for collective memory in which he distinguishes between communicative memory and cultural memory.[14] Communicative memory lies within the realm of living memory and everyday communication and is most usefully studied via the methods of oral history. It is characterised by ephemeral interactions and a high degree of formlessness and disorganisation. In contrast, cultural memory is bound to artefacts, relics, narratives and stories which operate as 'figures of memory',[15] temporally distant from a community but which offer a symbolic repository of memories that become gradually institutionalised and invested with meaning as a canon of accepted representations. Cultural memory, in this formulation, retains Halbwachs's vision of the individual enveloped by collective memory but addresses the force and potency of certain memories when those who experienced such events have disappeared. Cultural memory is, therefore, what occurs when memory is no longer lived by the community of those who remember but becomes overwhelmingly the preserve of archives, museums, rituals and cultural practices. It is here that fictional representations, such as crime fiction, may be positioned, as one element in a culture's system of self-representation that gains persistent cultural purchase over time.

Scholars of cultural memory work predominantly with these issues of representation, focusing on the cultural modelling of memory. As Katherine Hodgkin and Susannah Radstone contend, there is no such thing as unmediated memory: 'the past is constituted in narrative, always representation, always construction'.[16] Equally for Astrid Erll, 'individual memories are retrospective constructs'.[17] The study of cultural memory can, therefore, be conceived of as the examination of shared narrative constructions of the past, their conditions of reproduction in the present and their effects on contemporary and evolving cultural identities.[18] From this perspective, investigating cultural memory is not concerned with what happened in the past, examining truth claims from a variety of narrative sources, or investigating the empirical experience of the individual who engages with memory texts. Rather, it focuses upon how a culture, community or nation recognises itself in its visual and textual heritage and how that self-perception transforms in response to contemporary pressures and concerns.

For this model of cultural memory, as Wulf Kansteiner argues, 'it is crucial to keep in mind that all media of memory … neither simply reflect nor determine collective memory but are inextricably involved in its construction and evolution'.[19] Forms of representation are not, therefore, mere vessels of transmission but participate in the construction of meaning. In a similar vein, Ann Rigney analyses the cultural processes which allow memories to circulate in the contemporary era. These processes precondition what can be remembered and how, and determine which memories are appropriated and shared across groups. As a practice, Rigney identifies five distinguishing features in the contemporary workings of cultural memory. Firstly, cultural memory is a selective act of recall performed by members of a given community and whose memory work confers meaning on a particular set of memories. Secondly, cultural memory is based on principles of convergence. Rigney refers here to Pierre Nora's influential *lieux de mémoire* project as an incisive investigation of the ways in which a small number of real and virtual sites of memory become the locus of collective remembrance and historical significance. Thirdly, Rigney points to cultural memory as recursive, offering repeated patterns of representation across a variety of media which feed into one another and are powerfully linked to story-telling. Fourthly, cultural memory is dependent on narrative modelling for its communication, as successful transmission can be limited or facilitated by the availability of appropriate forms. Lastly, cultural memory offers opportunities for translation and transfer as new groups build upon previous cultural memories in order to legitimise their own claims to speak. In this expansive and open-ended model, Rigney makes a compelling case for cultural memory as practice and process in the present, not the recovery and recuperation of the past. Her model stresses the privileged role of artistic forms, such as the novel, as some of the most 'mobile media' of memory connecting communities.[20]

Fictional representations, such as novels, films, poems and plays, have long offered potent narratives for making the past accessible to the collective imagination. They have the potential to offer what Astrid Erll calls 'skeleton maps' of experience and remembering.[21] Fictional representations allow shared narratives of the past to move within and beyond memory communities in many of the ways outlined by Rigney. They rely on familiar story-telling conventions and models to convey memory;

they are highly adaptive and offer intermedial possibilities (for example novel to film adaptations) and they can inspire translation and transfer of memories across languages, cultures and traditions. Above all, what makes fictional representations so protean as a form of cultural memory is their interpretative variation. Fictional forms, such as the novel, can act as carriers of cultural memory that cannot be easily distilled into a particular memory formation. They offer sometimes discordant stories that suggest the multiplicity of interpretative possibilities for past events or experiences. This is evident in this study in Chapter 2 in which fictional representations of wartime Jewish persecution written in the 1950s and 1960s alternately recognise and deny the phenomenon of wartime anti-Semitism, thereby gesturing at the ambivalent status of such memories in the early post-war decades in France. As mediators of cultural memory, fictional forms have the potential to deepen our understanding of shared representations of the past in two important respects. Firstly, fictional forms can extend the scope and range of historical investigation, providing source material (records of opinions, attitudes and values) that can supplement more quantitative methods.[22] Secondly, they offer reflections on the afterlife of transformative events, such as war, and mould memory in different ways to other memory discourses, such as scholarly research or commemorative rituals. It is by examining the ways in which fictional forms, like the novel, operate a hold on the cultural imaginary that we can understand more about how collective experiences become embedded in social stories. Fictional forms and representations offer literary and cultural historians another route to map in a complex cartography of memory.

Memories of the Second World War: the case of France

War has been a particularly productive sphere for considering the construction of memory at the level of public and political discourses, as well as at the level of the individual and her or his experiences of suffering, mourning and remembrance. For Martin Evans, the presence of memory studies in war studies has been most visible following the 'cultural turn' in the 1990s. From a traditional understanding of war conceived of in terms of military strategy, great leaders and the technologies of war, the advent of memory studies has led to war being reconceptualised as a 'social and cultural phenomenon' that generates long-term legacies for both individuals and the collective.[23] This re-visioning of war has enabled a multi-faceted and critically informed model of war memories to evolve. This is well exemplified by the volume edited by T. G. Ashplant, Graham Dawson and Michael Roper on the politics of war memory and commemoration, above all in their introductory essay which charts war memories and their place in contemporary culture along three axes: narratives (shared representations of war), agencies (institutions and organisations, such as the nation-state, which direct or channel war memories) and arenas (socio-political spaces of war memory's transmission).[24] The innovation of this modelling is to explore war memories as the outcome of a diverse series of interactions, requiring an understanding of the narrative templates through which memories are constructed; the agents and actors who mobilise war memories and the socio-political contexts that confer meaning and ensure memories' circulation.

The Second World War in Europe is a major reference point for historians of memory. It was a conflict that generated unprecedented levels of material and human destruction. It was also a conflict that did not lend itself to the traditional language and models of post-conflict cultures, such as the First World War, which could be structured around a clear delineation of them and us and a divide between front-line operations and civilian life. Occupied nations, such as France, had to confront a mixed legacy of resistance bravery and submission to the occupier, while widespread castigation of Germany as the perpetrator nation in the early post-war years misrecognised significant levels of local support for its ideological agenda in the countries it had invaded. Nazi anti-Semitism tapped into home-grown traditions in various countries, such as Poland, and the years of German administration were a period when localised ethnic and political account-settling that had predated the war were tacitly accommodated. As the post-war period lengthened, the politics of the Cold War conditioned, distorted or, in some cases, silenced processes of remembrance and commemoration of the past. Such disrupted processes made it difficult for war narratives to emerge that could accommodate the diversity of individual, collective and national experiences of the Second World War.

Yet the war years and their memories were important in providing Western and Eastern European nations with the 'foundation myths' vital for post-war reconstruction.[25] In Western European nations, such as France, a selective set of war memories provided the public script for nation-building. These centred on the heroism of the Resistance, recast as a national movement of opposition to the occupier. Such an epic narrative legitimised and consolidated the power base of the ruling elites and would come to be mobilised as a political tool at moments of national crisis, such as the war in Algeria. This was not the only war narrative to gain purchase in the early post-war decades. As Alon Confino contends, perhaps the most powerful 'organising metaphor' for post-war memories of the Second World War was one of victimhood and martyrdom, a recasting of the recent past that made bearable the legacies of such a conflicted era.[26] With the unfreezing of Cold War relations, there came an explosive blast of reconnection to national and regional histories. In the West, and in France, this could be characterised as a process of democratisation as a more plural set of memory constructs were made visible in the public domain, enabling, for example, discussion of French state complicity in the Holocaust. In the countries of the former Eastern bloc, this release of war memories contributed to escalating national and inter-ethnic animosities that had been muted by the mantle of communist rule.[27] Even at fifty years distance, as Ashplant, Dawson and Roper assert: 'memories of the Second World War proved to have retained their power to shape current political identities, alignments and antagonisms'.[28]

The legacies of the Second World War are particularly complex in the case of France which, as an occupied country, has had to contend with a more divisive set of war memories than unambiguous war victors, such as Britain. In his major study of post-war memories of the Second World War, Henry Rousso coined the term the Vichy syndrome to identify the disparate social, political and cultural manifestations of the wartime past that have periodically surfaced in French public life. His study makes use of a psychoanalytical model and vocabulary, charting four phases in the evolution of French wartime memories. The first phase is one of 'unfinished mourning' (1944–54), where various political groupings vie for control of collective wartime memories. This is succeeded by a phase of 'repression' (1954–71), when a heroic war narrative of national resistance, identified largely with a Gaullist wartime perspective, is in the ascendancy, suppressing other more contentious group memories. There then comes a 'broken mirror' phase (1971–74), as collaboration and other darker memories re-emerge to fracture the resistance epic. The final phase, or rather the end point of the study first published in 1987, is a period of 'obsession' with a Jewish memory (above all French state complicity in the Holocaust) and the exploitation of the past for sectarian political purposes. In a second part, the study proceeds to illuminate this phasing of memory via analysis of three vectors or channels of memory: commemoration, cinema and historical research. Rousso ends by speculating on the state of a diffuse public memory of the war years and how it might relate to collective, if fluctuating, understandings of the past. In subsequent re-editions of this ground-breaking work, Rousso has underlined the heuristic value of the psychoanalytic vocabulary employed. However, even with such clarifications, the Vichy syndrome has now become shorthand for a memory condition that afflicts France as a nation and that may be applicable to subsequent conflicts in French collective memory, above all the Algerian War.

Rousso's model has proved influential for scholars of memory studies due to the critical attention the author pays to what might be perceived as the white noise of the Second World War in French public life. Rousso's model is attentive to the public narratives, agencies and arenas of war memory that have shaped French collective memory. Yet, Rousso's model of war memories is problematic when applied to fictional representations of the Second World War in two key respects. Firstly, his chronological model of memory evolution is not one that corresponds well to patterns of production in French fiction. As a number of critics have noted, French fictional representations of the war years, specifically the novel, do not necessarily follow a temporal phasing of silence, repression, return and obsession or the shift from memories of glorious resistance to the darker secrets of collaboration and Jewish persecution.[29] In the case of French fiction, a more fluid model is required that takes account of 'waves of reworking the past' and the repeated depictions of culturally resonant war experiences, such as civilian suffering or the compromises of resistance.[30] This notion of the patterning of memory opens the way for a more fine-grained cultural history of war memories than the metanarratives of the Vichy syndrome might allow.

Secondly, Rousso's model pays insufficient attention to the media of memory. While filmic representations are discussed in the study, this takes the form of a broad survey, charting periods of 'fever' or 'remission' in film production, rather than a detailed analysis of individual film genres and their particular recasting of the past. However, as Ashplant, Dawson and Roper emphasise in their work, understanding the 'micro-politics of aesthetic form' is essential when approaching war memories and their evolution. In their modelling of war memories, well-established and familiar narrative templates have the power to create a space for hidden or unassimilated memories; to prepare the ground for political expression; and even to provide possibilities for understanding what is not yet in the public domain.[31] Rousso's 'public, often official, and narrowly political memory', as Alon Confino terms it, runs, therefore, the risk of underestimating the formative role of more diffuse social and cultural vectors of memory, such as popular fiction, and their potential to generate discussion, debate and dissent.[32] An intriguing example of crime fiction's ability to influence the processes of war memory transmission is offered by Didier Daeninckx's *Meurtres pour mémoire* (1984), a crime novel credited with galvanising the campaign to have former Vichy civil servant, Maurice Papon, tried for wartime crimes against humanity. Interweaving references to the complicity of the French state in the Holocaust and the bloody police repression of a demonstration on 17 October 1961 at the height of the Algerian War, Daeninckx's popular fiction harnessed the generic conventions of crime fiction (perpetration, guilt, responsibility and justice) for a controversial exposé of Papon, whose wartime and post-war administrative career mirrored that of his fictional counterpart in the novel. By exploiting the investigative structure of crime fiction, Daeninckx (whose novel is discussed in Chapter 3) offered a polemical cultural intervention in memory debates, bringing popular culture into direct confrontation with politics and justice. Such an example demonstrates the richness and multiplicity of memory discourses in circulation beyond the realm of politics and political actors and the role of popular culture as one significant vector of memory.

Popular culture: the case of crime fiction

The study of popular culture encompasses an extraordinarily diverse range of artefacts and social processes. For Dominic Strinati, the object of study, popular culture, is determined largely by the theoretical traditions in which it is framed.[33] Critical approaches range from the work of mass culture critics who define popular culture as 'folk culture' in preindustrial societies or mass-produced culture in industrial societies; to the Frankfurt School, which perceives popular culture as cultural forms produced by the cultural industry in order to secure the continuity of capitalism; to more recent postmodernist perspectives that analyse popular culture as embodying radical changes in the role of the mass media which erode the distinction between image and reality. However, the linkage between popular culture, the mass media and conservative social and aesthetic values is a persistent one, informing a common-sense view that forms of popular culture, such as fiction, film, television and popular music, are 'little more than a degraded culture, successfully imposed from above, to make profit and secure ideological control'.[34] This study approaches popular culture quite differently, influenced by the work of British cultural studies theorists, such as Stuart Hall. From this theoretical perspective, culture is defined politically rather than aesthetically, as a 'key site for the production and reproduction of the social relations of everyday life'.[35] For John Storey, cultural studies grounded in a Marxist analysis offers two key interventions for understanding popular culture: firstly, that cultural texts or practices must be analysed in relation to their social and historical conditions of production and consumption. Popular fiction does not mimetically transpose the structure and shape of history but is part of history's processes and practices. Secondly, that culture is a site of struggle for meaning; that within and through cultural productions, such as popular fiction, competing and subordinate groups can attempt to resist the imposition of meanings which serve the interest of dominant groups. This resistance is not always successful and consumers of popular culture are not always empowered by their textual encounters. However, this is not to deny the transformative potential of popular culture, caught up in a dialectical exchange between the processes of production and activities of consumption that have the power to shape how people think about the world around them. Crime fiction is one form of popular culture acutely responsive to such possibilities.

As a global phenomenon, crime fiction is an extremely mobile form of popular culture and has made inroads into world literatures from Europe and America to Sub-Saharan Africa, Japan and Australasia.[36] The transnational adaptability of crime fiction may stem, paradoxically, from its very constraints as a set of sub-genres; broadly speaking, the whodunit, the thriller and the suspense novel. These are bound to a set of aesthetic conventions but have generated myriad reconfigurations. Indeed, in the French context, forms of detective and crime fiction have offered fertile terrain for literary experimentation, as well as socio-political critique. From the beginnings of detective and crime fiction in the mid-nineteenth century, France has been at the forefront of developments, one of the three founding cultures whose literary cross-fertilisation led to the genesis of early narrative models of detection and investigation.[37] Crime fiction has also, in France, been the subject of legitimate critical analysis from the early twentieth century and accommodated a wide range of readings: from genre studies and narratology to psychoanalysis and post-structuralism.[38] These have generated important insights that have been influential far beyond crime fiction itself. In more recent decades, academic criticism has taken a 'cultural turn', with crime fiction cast as a formative narrative for understanding cultural histories of postwar France.[39] The present study falls squarely into such a critical framing of crime fiction. Crime fiction here will be approached as a narrative form that engages with the struggles to understand the social, political and moral conflicts and dilemmas that the Second World War has bequeathed France as a nation.

The cultural resonance between crime fiction and cultural memories of the Second World War in France is not confined to French authors. British and American authors, particularly since the 1990s, have been drawn to depict the political, ideological and, above all, moral dilemmas of French resistance and collaboration, as well as the post-war legacies of occupation. In *A Good Death* (2000), Elizabeth Ironside builds her crime narrative upon the internal schisms and factionalism of wartime resistance made visible in the immediate aftermath of war in the small commune of Lepech Pedrissou in southern France.[40] In his best-selling series of espionage novels set during the inter-war and war years in Europe, Alan Furst devotes *The World at Night* (1998) to the hesitant beginnings of resistance for an upper-class film producer, Jean Casson, who becomes a reluctant spy for the Germans and then a resistance network in order to save his lover and secure his own survival if not freedom in occupied Paris.[41] In relation to collaboration, Brian Moore, in *The Statement* (1995), offers a fictionalised reworking of the post-war itinerary of a Paul Touvier-like character, a wartime militia leader with strong anti-Semitic beliefs who is harboured by the Catholic Church with his family for much of the post-war period.[42] As with the novels of Ironside and Furst, *The Statement* focuses upon the complex nature of wartime allegiances and, in this case, their reverberations in the contemporary era. These novels all beg the question of what makes this cultural connection between France, the Second World War and crime fiction so compelling for authors and readers, both within and beyond France. Why does crime fiction offer such an apposite vehicle for re-examining France's wartime past?

The connections can be attributed to three factors: firstly, the cultural politics of crime fiction. Crime fiction, above all in its *noir* incarnation, constructs a narrative that revolves around crimes and transgressions never fully resolved, leaving a residue of uncertainty and fear that undermines the reassurance of closure. In the *noir* universe, doomed antiheroes engage in the pursuit of justice and truth that rarely succeeds and the predominant tone is one of the failures of collective endeavours and a misplaced trust in authority and order. This is a moral universe of shades of grey and where right and wrong are relative concepts. Projected onto the war years in France, this narrative vision inevitably accentuates the fallibility (indeed culpability) of the Vichy regime, the brutalities of the

German occupation and its French agents, such as the militia, and the pervasive surveillance, persecution and arbitrary violence of a period that moves from defeat and occupation to liberation and civil war. The established order is criminal and those who oppose it are exposed to betrayal, injustice and terror. Such a vision is evident in the crime novels examined in Chapter 1, which deconstruct heroic visions of resistance in favour of a morally conflicted view of collective indifference, powerlessness and violence under occupation. Projected onto the post-war period and memories of war, this vision highlights selective silences and secret histories that enable some war stories to circulate, above all the resistance epic, and others to be occluded. Unearthing such counter-histories of war is characteristic of crime fictions centred on second-generation protagonists, such as the children of collaborators dramatised in Georges-Jean Arnaud's *Maudit Blood* (1985) discussed in Chapter 3. The cultural politics of crime fiction constructs, therefore, a memory of war marked by strategies of contestation. These strategies tend to fragment monolithic war narratives in an attempt to render the human motivations and subjective experiences of history.

Secondly, the productive intersections of crime fiction and the war years can be attributed to the fact that crime fiction approaches the past in the mode of an investigation. All sub-genres of crime fiction call upon the reader to adopt a suspicious stance and to question and mistrust what is presented as social fact in favour of a more nuanced reading of social reality.[43] Narrators can be unreliable; power relations hidden and the truth, provisional and even a chimera. In many of the later crime fictions discussed in this study, such a narrative framing of the past generates a history from below, as an ordinary protagonist, not one of the powerbrokers of history, undertakes a quest for knowledge. This representation of the past is demonstrated in Chapter 4 in three novels which depict main protagonists charged with uncovering a lost history of the Holocaust and the concentration camps. As Elfriede Müller and Alexandre Ruoff argue in their short study of French crime fiction and history, the individual crime in the present poses questions and unsettles received views of recent conflicts in which France has played a role.[44] Crime fiction offers, therefore, an interpretative frame for the Second World War that opens up the past to interrogation and, in later fictions, to the ethical imperative to confront the past and take collective responsibility.

Lastly, the coupling of the Second World War and crime fiction allows authors to sketch out the complex processes of memory, individual, collective and cultural. Crime fiction is a narrative built upon the imperative to track traces of the past (the crime) in the present and thereby to locate the source of disorder. The fallibility, falsity and innate unpredictability of memory are central conceits for crime fiction structured around an investigation into troubled personal and national histories and their reverberations in the present. In the case of French crime fiction and the Second World War, it is striking how far its narrative universe is peopled with characters marked indelibly by the past and overwhelmed by memories of war. These maimed memory people range from the figure of the amnesiac in the fiction of authors, such as Léo Malet and Patrick Pécherot,[45] to the children and grandchildren of those who survived the war years and contend with the traumatic legacy of resistance and collaboration or racial persecution, deportation and extermination. Indeed questions of familial and generational transmission of memory are central to recent French crime fiction as successor generations attempt to grapple with what the historical record has retained and what may have been silenced or marginalised. This quest for knowledge of the wartime past is explored in novels for younger readers discussed in Chapter 5, which pivot upon memories of Jewish persecution and the figure of the lost child. Crime fiction as memory text, therefore, suggests the continuing memory troubles of war and war's potential to influence contemporary social relations and identities.

Parameters and methods

This study will examine cultural memories of the Second World War in selected French crime fiction published from the late 1940s to the 2010s. In terms of its parameters, it will focus on novels published in specialist series marketed and distributed as crime fiction, such as Editions Gallimard's Série noire, or produced by authors identified closely with popular crime-writing traditions. It will not investigate more general prose fiction that makes use of a crime intrigue. This is not to underestimate the cultural significance of such a body of fiction. Fictions which exploit crime conventions to animate political and moral debates on the legacies of the Second World War have much to offer the reader and the scholar.[46] This study has a different aim: to analyse the war narratives of novels that are purposely situated in traditions of detective and crime fiction and that make use of such narrative templates to construct particular formulations of French war memories which, it will be argued, merit scrutiny.[47] Within the corpus of crime fiction available, the study will focus on novels that use the occupation or war years as the narrative motor of the text. This may be by situating events during the Second World War itself, a form of *histoire en directe*, or by making use of the war years as an epicentre of transgression which reaches into the narrative present. Cultural representations of the Second World War will be examined at the level of plot, for example in relation to character motivation and interactions, and as discursive strategies that may include thematic preoccupations, the use of metaphor and analogy or intertextual references to, for example, other historical events, such as France's wars of decolonisation.

As a study situated within cultural studies, the working methodologies of this book are threefold. Firstly, it will argue that fictional representations of the war years are inextricably connected to the social and cultural fabric of the time of writing. They will be approached as the products of shared recollection and reconstruction in the present that cannot be separated from collective memories within which authors, as agents of memory, are situated. The book will, therefore, provide an integrated discussion of a selection of crime fictions from the late 1940s to the 2010s, reading the crime novels contextually, as both reflective of and participatory in the memory discourses in circulation at the time of their composition. Secondly, it will argue that, in order to study the cultural memories of war, it is vital to analyse the narrative templates that regulate the transmission of memory. In the case of crime fiction, this revolves around a cultural politics of contestation, an investigative mode of addressing the past and a preoccupation with the processes of memory and questions of guilt, culpability, responsibility and justice. Thirdly, this book will assert that French crime fiction, as popular culture, is a site of consent and resistance to dominant histories of the past. The crime novels selected for study will be analysed as offering important cultural interventions as part of a broader memorial landscape of the Second World War that is in constant evolution. The aim will be to position examples of crime fiction as memory texts amongst a cluster of other shared cultural reconstructions of the past that can shed new light on the evolution of French memories of the Second World War.

This modelling of cultural memory has been translated into the following chapter organisation. Chapter 1 focuses on representations of resisters and the Resistance in crime fiction of the late 1940s and early 1950s, a period when the resistance epic of national heroism was being consecrated as the dominant war memory underpinning post-war French reconstruction. This chapter investigates the violent and highly polemical contestation of such a vision in the work of three French crime writers and their alternative focus on resistance fracture, violence and victimhood. In Chapter 2, discussion moves to the 1950s and 1960s, a period often characterised as given over to an apparent forgetting of the negative national legacies of the war years, such as French collaboration and the persecution of the Jews. This chapter identifies, in sharp counterpoint, the presence of such forgotten crimes in French crime fiction and their representation via the trope of Jewish auto-denunciation. In Chapter 3, the analytical viewpoint shifts to the resurgence of collaboration in fiction of the 1970s and 1980s. This chapter examines the work of three French crime novelists and assesses the extent to which their popular re-casting of collaboration as a collective, systemic phenomenon builds upon the pioneering work of a new generation of French and American historians of the Vichy regime and collaboration. Chapter 4 looks to representations of the concentration camps and the figure of the survivor-witness in French crime fiction of the 1980s and 1990s. These fictions were produced at a time of increasing visibility of France's wartime past with the trials for crimes against humanity of former Vichy figures, such as Maurice Papon. The chapter argues for a change in approach in French crime fiction about the Second World War as hybrid forms – both creative reconstruction and historical documentation – allow a wave of younger novelists to dramatise what it means to confront war memories as the successor generation. Lastly, Chapter 5 investigates cultural memories of the Second World War for younger readers of the 1990s and 2000s. Concerned predominantly with the memory of the persecution of the Jews in France, specifically the infamous round-ups of 16 July 1942, these novels demonstrate, in parallel with other vectors of memory such as the classroom, the extent to which memories of the Second World War are being mobilised today as civic memories intended to inform and instruct new generations of French men and women. The study will end with a brief discussion of war memories past, present and future and the main conclusions to be drawn from the corpus of novels studied.

In this book, crime fiction is read as a body of work that extends our knowledge of the cultural matrix shaping memories of the Second World War in France. It stands as a popular manifestation of the complex interactions of history, memory and culture and gives a distinctive and morally charged colouration (crime, guilt and responsibility) to the study of collective memories that continue to haunt the French cultural imaginary.[48] As the examination of French crime fiction in this book will demonstrate, what can often pass largely unobserved – crime fiction as the infra-ordinary of literary production – has the potential to offer intriguing insights into the plural and evolving memory discourses of war and to further our understanding of 'un passé qui ne passe pas'.[49]

Notes

1   Didier Daeninckx, *La Mémoire longue, textes et images 1986–2008* (Paris: Le Cherche-Midi, 2008), p. 215 (the heaviest suitcase on a journey is the invisible one which contains memories).

2   This term is taken from Olivier Wieviorka's *La Mémoire désunie: le souvenir politique des années sombres de la Libération à nos jours* (Paris: Editions du Seuil, 2010).

3   'Introduction', Edric Caldicott and Anne Fuchs (eds), *Cultural Memory: Essays on European Literature and History* (Bern: Peter Lang, 2003), pp. 11–32 (p. 12).

4   See, for example, Avishia Margalit, *The Ethics of Memory* (Cambridge, MA: Harvard University Press, 2002).

5   Jan-Werner Muller, 'Introduction: the power of memory, the memory of power and the power over memory', in Jan-Werner Muller (ed.), *Memory and Power in Post-War Europe: Studies of the Presence of the Past* (Cambridge: Cambridge University Press, 2002), pp. 1–38.

6   See, for example, Shoshana Felman and Dori Laub, *Testimony: Crises of Witnessing in Literature, Psychoanalysis and History* (London: Routledge, 1992).

7   Popular Memory Group, 'Popular memory: theory, politics, method', in Richard Johnson, Gregor McLennan, Bill Schwarz and David Sutton (eds), *Making Histories: Studies in History-Writing and Politics* (London: Hutchinson University Library, 1982), pp. 205–52 (p. 211).

8   Ann Rigney, 'Plenitude, scarcity and the circulation of cultural memory', *Journal of European Studies*, 35:1 (2005), 11–28 (14).

9   Katherine Hodgkin and Susannah Radstone, 'Introduction', in Katherine Hodgkin and Susannah Radstone (eds), *Memory, History, Nation: Contested Pasts* (New Brunswick/London: Transaction Publishers, 2007), pp. 1–22 (p. 5).

10   This definition of memory discourses is derived from the introduction to Katharina Hall and Kathryn N. Jones (eds), *Constructions of Conflict: Transmitting Memories of the Past in European Historiography, Culture and Media* (Bern: Peter Lang, 2011), pp. 1–14 (p. 5).

11   Maurice Halbwachs, *On Collective Memory*, edited and translated by Lewis A. Coser (London/Chicago: University of Chicago Press, 1992), p. 43.

12   Halbwachs, *On Collective Memory*, p. 49.

13   Historian Mary Fulbrook has recently developed these insights in order to investigate further the relationship between the inner voice of the individual, what might be termed the authenticity of experience, and its relationship

to the outer social frame of collective memory. See Fulbrook, 'Patterns of Memory', in Hall and Jones (eds), *Constructions of Conflict*, pp. 17–33.

14   Jan Assmann, 'Collective memory and cultural identity', *New German Critique*, 65 (1995), 125–33.

15   Assmann, 'Collective memory and cultural identity', 129.

16   Hodgkin and Radstone, *Memory, History, Nation*, p. 2.

17   Astrid Erll, 'Wars we have seen: literature as a medium of collective memory in the "age of extremes"', in Elena Lamberti and Vita Fortunati (eds), *Memories and Representations of War: The Case of World War One and World War Two* (Amsterdam: Rodopi, 2009), pp. 27–43 (p. 32).

18   Definitions of cultural memory converge on notions of representation and identity but differ in terms of their emphasis. For Caldicott and Fuchs, questions of narrative form are paramount: 'cultural memory can be understood as a repertoire of symbolic forms and stories through which communities advance or edit competing identities', 'Introduction', *Cultural Memory, Essays on European Literature and History*, p. 18. For Elena Lamberti, the focus is on issues of heritage and national framing: 'a heritage that each nation has created over time in order to mould its own identity', 'Introduction', *Memories and Representations of War*, p. 3.

19   Wulf Kansteiner, 'Finding meaning in memory: a methodological critique of collective memory', *History and Theory*, 41:2 (2001), 179–97 (195).

20   Rigney, 'Plenitude, scarcity and the circulation of cultural memory', 20.

21   Erll, 'Wars we have seen', p. 32.

22   In *Collaboration and Resistance in Occupied France: Representing Treason and Sacrifice* (Basingstoke: Palgrave/Macmillan, 2003), Christopher Lloyd argues that 'personal testimony and fictional reconstruction are indispensable to historical understanding; indeed, there are many aspects of war and occupation that can be understood *only* through works that convey subjective experience' (p. 5).

23   Martin Evans, 'Opening up the battlefield: war studies and the cultural turn', *Journal of War and Culture Studies*, 1:1 (2008), 47–51 (49).

24   'The politics of war memory and commemoration: contexts, structures and dynamics', in T. G. Ashplant, Graham Dawson and Michael Roper (eds), *The Politics of War Memory and Commemoration* (London: Routledge, 2000), pp. 3–85.

25   Tony Judt, 'The past is another country: myth and memory in post-war Europe', in Jan-Werner Muller (ed.), *Memory and Power in Post-War Europe: Studies of the Presence of the Past* (Cambridge: Cambridge University Press, 2002), pp. 157–83 (p. 168).

26   Alon Confino, 'Remembering the Second World War, 1945–1965: narratives of victimhood and genocide', *Cultural Analysis*, 4 (2005), 46–75 (48).

27   The legacies of the war in the Balkans are illustrated by the capture, on 27 May 2011, of former Serbian General, Ratko Mladic, responsible for the

1995 Srebrenica massacre, and his imminent trial at the UN war crimes tribunal in The Hague.

28 'The politics of war memory and commemoration: contexts, structures and dynamics', in Ashplant, Dawson and Roper (eds), *The Politics of War Memory*, p. 64.

29 In his study of French occupation fiction from 1945 to the present, Michel Jacquet notes that there was not a sudden recovery of memories of collaboration in French fiction in the 1970s but rather continuity of representation. See Jacquet, *Une occupation très romanesque: ironie et dérision dans le roman français sur l'occupation de 1945 à nos jours* (Paris: Les Editions La Bruyère, 2000), pp. 6–7. In a similar vein, Michael L. Berkvam contends that a Gaullist view of the war years is absent from much French war fiction of the immediate post-war decades. See Berkvam, *Writing the Story of France in World War II: Literature and Memory 1942–1958* (New Orleans: University Press of the South, 2000), p. xvii.

30 Helmut Peitsch, 'Studying European literary memories', in Helmut Peitsch, Charles Burdett and Claire Gorrara (eds), *European Memories of the Second World War* (Oxford: Berghahn Books, 1999), pp. xiii–xxxi (p. xxxi).

31 'The politics of war memory and commemoration', in Ashplant, Dawson, Roper (eds), *The Politics of War Memory*, pp. 36–9.

32 Alon Confino, 'Memory and cultural history: problems of method', *The American Historical Review*, 102:5 (1997), 1386–1403 (1394).

33 Dominic Strinati, *An Introduction to Theories of Popular Culture* (London: Routledge, 2004).

34 John Storey, *Cultural Studies and the Study of Popular Culture* (Edinburgh: Edinburgh University Press, 1996), p. 6.

35 Storey, *Cultural Studies and the Study of Popular Culture*, p. 2.

36 This is reflected in the surge of public interest in international crime fiction in the last decade and its scholarly corollary. See, for example, Marieke Krajenbrink and Kate M. Quinn (eds), *Investigating Identities: Questions of Identity in Contemporary International Crime Fiction* (Amsterdam: Rodopi, 2009), Christine Matzke and Susanne Mühleisen (eds), *Postcolonial Postmortems: Crime Fiction from a Transcultural Perspective* (Amsterdam: Rodopi, 2006) and Nels Pearson and Marc Singer (eds), *Detective Fiction in a Postcolonial and Transnational World* (Farnham: Ashgate, 2009). The transatlantic connections between American and francophone African crime fiction are examined in Pim Higginson, *The Noir Atlantic: Chester Himes and the Birth of the Francophone African Crime Novel* (Liverpool: Liverpool University Press, 2011).

37 See David Platten, 'Origins and beginnings: the emergence of detective fiction', in Claire Gorrara (ed.), *French Crime Fiction* (Cardiff: University of Wales Press, 2009), pp. 14–35.

38 Some of the most influential studies include: Roger Callois' 'Puissances du

roman', in *Approches de l'imaginaire* (Paris: Gallimard, 1974), pp. 177–205, first published in 1941 (form and genre); Tzvetan Todorov, 'A typology of detective fiction', in *The Poetics of Prose*, trans. Richard Howard (Oxford: Blackwells, 1977), pp. 42–54 (narratology); Francis Lacassin, *Mythologies du roman policier* (Paris: UGE, 1974) (literary and cultural history); Roland Barthes, *S/Z* (Paris: Editions du Seuil, 1976) (structuralism); and Jacques Lacan's seminar on Poe's 'The Purloined Letter', reproduced in *Ecrits* (Paris: Editions du Seuil, 1966) (post-structuralism).

39   See, for example, *French Cultural Studies*, 12:3 (2001) devoted to discourses of crime and punishment in French social and cultural history, *Yale French Studies*, 108 (2005), devoted to 'Crime Fictions' and Claire Gorrara, *The Roman Noir in Post-War French Culture: Dark Fictions* (Oxford: Oxford University Press, 2003).

40   Elizabeth Ironside, *A Good Death* (London: Hodder & Stoughton, 2000).

41   Alan Furst, *The World at Night* (London: HarperCollins Publishers, 1998).

42   Brian Moore, *The Statement* (London: Bloomsbury Publishing, 1995).

43   See Jean Pons, 'Le roman noir, littérature réelle', in *Les Temps modernes*, 595 (August–October 1997), 5–14, for a reading of crime fiction as a means of interrogating social reality.

44   Elfriede Müller and Alexandre Ruoff, *Le Polar français: crime et histoire* (Paris: La Fabrique Editions, 2002).

45   In Léo Malet's *120, rue de la gare* (1943), an amnesiac prisoner-of-war triggers the crime intrigue and introduces the reader to Malet's private detective, Nestor Burma. The narrative catalyst of a psychologically troubled victim and memory disturbance is repeated in Patrick Pécherot, *Boulevard des Branques* (Paris: Gallimard, 2005), set during the occupation and the third in his Nestor Burma mysteries in homage to Malet's detective.

46   A major AHRC-funded project devoted to prose narratives of the Second World War in France since 1939, led by Professors Margaret Atack and Christopher Lloyd, has just been completed and provides the researcher with a current thematic and bibliographical database of over 1,000 texts, including entries for eighty-six detective and crime fiction novels. See www. frame.leeds.ac.uk/database (accessed 28 July 2011).

47   I am aware of the need to gauge the reception (or consumption) of cultural representations of the past as a means of understanding how, and if, a given textual production responded to widely circulating views of the wartime past. Within this study, I do not intend to provide quantitative data, for example sales figures, to advance claims over consumption. Such figures do not necessarily equate to whether a reader endorsed a given representation. It may be that the genre (crime fiction) predisposed purchase rather than the subject matter (war). Rather, I will provide information on the number and timing of re-editions of a novel discussed, using this as a barometer of how the publishing industry, as a prime vector of memory, positively

judged the correlation of a text with the collective war memories of the day.

48 The Vichy regime as a spectre haunting the French present is used as a rhetorical device in Richard Golsan's *Vichy's Afterlife: History and Counterhistory in Postwar France* (Lincoln, NE: Nebraska University Press, 2000) whose introduction is entitled 'The Body in the Basement'.

49 Eric Conan and Henry Rousso, *Vichy, un passé qui ne passe pas* (Paris: Editions Fayard, 1994).

~1~

Resisters and the resistance: challenging the epic in French crime fiction of the 1940s and 1950s

Paris! Paris outragé! Paris brisé! Paris martyrisé! Mais Paris libéré! Libéré pas lui-même, libéré par son peuple avec le concours des armées de la France, avec l'appui et le concours de la France tout entière, de la France qui se bat, de la seule France, de la vraie France, de la France éternelle![1]

On 25 August 1944, at the Paris *Hôtel de Ville*, General Charles de Gaulle laid the cornerstone for one of the most influential war narratives of French occupation and liberation. To an acclaiming crowd, de Gaulle constructed a glorious image of a nation of resisters who had risen from the ashes of defeat to free themselves from German tyranny. Now resurgent, France was ready to reclaim its place on the world stage as a victor, rather than a victim, of the Second World War. In the succeeding months and years, an idealised construction of resistance, later to be termed the *résistancialiste* myth, was incorporated into the foundation myths of France. It provided a 'kind of patriotic epic that only the Resistance could deliver'[2] and has become synonymous with a war narrative of national heroism that has retained its appeal into the twenty-first century.[3]

This chapter will examine this epic narrative of resistance and challenges to its cultural ascendancy in the work of three French crime writers: Jean Meckert, André Héléna and Gilles Morris. It will argue that this cultural projection of war in the 1940s and 1950s masked a more plural set of war memories that, in the case of crime fiction, took the form of antagonistic stories of resistance infighting, violence and marginalisation. The chapter will begin, therefore, by setting out the resistance epic of the late 1940s and early 1950s. It will analyse the national and political values at stake in its mobilisation and its incarnation in the figure of the male resistance fighter. It will then examine narratives that contested such a vision of wartime heroism, above all the counter-narratives of French fiction which highlighted the moral ambiguities of life under occupation. It will focus in particular on the *roman noir*, discussing its potential as a vehicle for critical commentary on the war years and the legacies of the Resistance. Finally, the chapter will explore strategies of contestation in novels by Meckert, Héléna and Morris and assess how these *noir* authors present resisters in a different light to the official discourse of bravery and sacrifice. These are war stories of protagonists estranged from the national narrative of common struggle. They reflect upon one of the major tensions of French war memories of the early post-war years: the mismatch between the Resistance as a mythic construct and the multiple histories and experiences of resisters as individuals.

Constructing the resistance epic

The resistance epic of the early post-war years was an assertion of national fortitude and valour. This epic war story declared that France had resisted the occupier and that the general population had been complicit if not actively engaged in the national struggle. Resisters themselves were represented as heroes who had sacrificed their lives to defend the Republican values of *liberté*, *égalité* and *fraternité*. The divisions and disagreements between the external (the London-based Gaullist Free French) and the internal resistance were presented as an obstacle overcome in the common pursuit of national liberation. In such a war narrative, de Gaulle emerged as the self-proclaimed embodiment of French sovereignty during wartime, a figure who had denied the authority of Vichy and asserted the existence of a fighting France in the face of Allied suspicions and mistrust. Pivotal to this war narrative were claims to military prowess, above all the contribution of the internal and external resistance to the liberation of French territory.[4] As Henri Michel, an early post-war historian of the Resistance, would assert, the adventure of resistance 'constitue un des plus magnifiques épisodes de l'histoire de la France'.[5]

This resistance epic was certainly more than a political discourse. It was embedded in the social, cultural and political values of immediate post-war France. It was sanctioned in the attribution of medals for resistance heroism, above all in de Gaulle's personal nomination of 1,036 *Compagnons de la Libération*, disproportionately awarded to members of the Free French.[6] It was performed in the unveiling of plaques and statues to resistance heroes and victims of German aggression. It was consecrated in national ceremonies, such as that inaugurated at Mont Valérien on 11 November 1945, site of more than 1,000 executions of resisters by firing squad.[7] It was celebrated in film and fiction, perhaps most emblematically in Vercors' wartime short story 'Le Silence de la mer' (1942), an allegory of passive resistance in which an uncle and niece oppose the seductive monologue of the German officer billeted to their home with an implacable silence. It was endorsed politically with over 80 per cent of the Constituent Assembly of 1945 belonging to political parties that claimed to speak for the Resistance.[8] In a very real sense, therefore, accepting such a narrative of national resistance conferred political power. It established the authority of the post-war ruling elites and justified their moral claims to lead post-war reconstruction. It provided the benchmark values for the transition to democracy. Externally, it provided a platform for the exercise of international power and prestige. With its resistance credentials intact, France could claim a place at the banquet of the victors and influence the new world order.

The most potent carrier of such an epic narrative of resistance in these early post-war years was the male resister, or rather an idealised vision of male wartime activism. Such a figure came in a number of guises, all of which drew on popular cultural images of the warrior-hero. For resistance historian Henri Michel, he is drawn in the likeness of the clandestine operative, one of the shadow army who is willing to pay for his beliefs with the ultimate sacrifice of his life. This vision is powerfully evoked in Joseph Kessel's resistance novel, *L'Armée des ombres* of 1943, brought to the cinema screen in *film noir* tones in 1969 by Jean-Pierre Melville.[9] For later historians, such as Luc Capdevila, the masculine archetype of these early post-war years is the armed volunteer, above all the *maquis* fighter who had taken to the countryside or mountains to avoid capture or the labour draft, and who asserted his power and authority via a virile brotherhood of arms.[10] This iconography of masculine prowess was promoted in the early post-war years in poster form. It offered a sharp counterpoint to the press photographs of the *tondues*. These were women suspected of relations with the occupier and who had been forcibly shorn of their hair in a ritualistic display of gendered humiliation and punishment at the Liberation.[11] Such figures pointed to a very different set of war memories and war narratives in circulation in the late 1940s and early 1950s.

Counter-narratives, counter-fictions

The resistance epic, as war narrative, was inevitably highly selective and partisan and distorted the multiple histories and trajectories of occupation and liberation. As Pierre Nora argues, France, in the immediate aftermath of war, was a country that could more properly be described as half-victor, half-vanquished.[12] This was a nation that had lived through military defeat, territorial partition, social breakdown, economic hardship, persecutions, mass deportations and a bloody civil war of liberation, and was still in the grips of a 'un règlement de comptes familial et idéologique'.[13] Nora's schizophrenic vision of France and the war years, victor and vanquished at one and the same time, underscores the fact that no war story could hope to represent such a diversity of experiences and memories. Indeed, any patriotic epic that purported to do so was open to challenge and contestation. For, while the battles for national liberation raged across late 1944 and early 1945, other histories of the recent past were already jostling for public recognition; from the particular heroism of the French Communist Party to the claims by supporters of the Vichy regime that they had defended French interests in the face of German demands.[14] The most persistent alternative to the resistance epic in these years was a war narrative of national suffering.

Certainly, what might now be perceived as the pendant to resistance heroism, civilian suffering, was the common experience of many French people during the occupation. In his study of memories of the Second World War in France, Belgium and the Netherlands, Pieter Lagrou comments that the key word in the immediate post-war decades was deportation rather than resistance. Deportation to labour camps, internment camps or concentration and extermination camps was the fate of more than two million men, women and children resident in France. Deportation encompassed the experience of those deported for acts of resistance, political opponents of Vichy and the Germans and others classified as undesirables. It included those conscripted to work in Germany under the national labour scheme, voluntary and forced, prisoners of war and those persecuted on racial or ethnic grounds, above all the Jewish population. This listing alone illustrates how deportation affected almost every strata of French society. It 'epitomised the experience of French society better than any phrase, and certainly better than *Résistance*'.[15]

But were these experiences visible in the public sphere in these early post-war years? A number of historians and literary critics point to a dearth of such war narratives in the late 1940s. They attributed this to two factors: the reluctance of returnees themselves to tell their stories and the lack of receptivity to such narratives of suffering; people were already fatigued by their own experiences of wartime hardships at home and scarcely able to process the stories of others.[16] Yet, war narratives of deportation are evident, if fleeting, in French fiction and film of these years. Simone de Beauvoir's 1945 novel, *Le Sang des autres*, depicts the main female protagonist, Hélène Bertrand, witnessing the heart-rending separation of a mother and child in the round-up of Jews in Paris in 1942. In Beauvoir's later *Les Mandarins* of 1954, characters remember Jewish friends who disappeared, making explicit reference to the Paris internment camp of Drancy.[17] In the co-directed film, *Retour à la vie* (1949), the problematic homecoming of five prisoners of war and one Jewish concentration camp deportee is represented as a gruelling and painful process of reintegration into post-war French society. Indeed, as Margaret Atack asserts, what emerges from broader studies of French fiction of the 1950s is that writers 'far from endorsing a story of heroic resistance and a united nation, foreground confusion, division and moral complexity ...'.[18] Atack's research underscores the extent to which many novels of the period paint a picture of the cruel and competing interests of occupation, covering supposedly taboo topics, such as collaboration, the black market, anti-Semitism and collective indifference to the suffering of others. In this context, resistance heroism is debunked as shallow self-interest or pathological otherness, with resistance merely one option amongst others when faced with the compromises and choices of life under German and Vichy rule. Such morally ambivalent depictions of the occupation and resistance can be traced in French crime fiction of this period, particularly in the form of the *roman noir*.

Noir visions of war

The convergence of the French *roman noir* and *les années noires* is one grounded in the ethics and poetics of hard-boiled crime fiction.[19] Pioneered by American and British inter-war writers, such as Raymond Chandler and Dashiell Hammett, the hard-boiled format was given a new lease of life by French writers with the launch of Gallimard's now iconic Série noire in 1945 under the editorship of former surrealist Marcel Duhamel. For the first time, Duhamel collected under one label a disparate set of American and British detective and crime fiction that had received little critical attention in their home cultures. Via their translation, he gave them a literary cachet and counter-cultural status that would see them feted in the French literary world and circulated in other European countries under the label of the *roman noir*.[20] Exported back to the United States following such critical acclaim, a new genre was invented that would gain worldwide appeal, both in novel and filmic form.

What made the *roman noir* such an attractive form for French, and increasingly European, authors in the post-war period was its disabused narrative of modernity, often projected onto a darkly dystopian cityscape. As Raymond Chandler was to note in his 1944 essay on 'the simple art of murder', realistic crime fiction, in the mould of Dashiell Hammett's novels, 'took murder out of the Venetian vase and dropped it into the alley'.[21] These were stories of the corruption and excesses of the urban metropolis where trust in law and order had broken down and civilised values were but a thin veneer for greed, venality and cruelty. The detective in such fictions was an honourable man, but not a model of unimpeachable virtue, and duplicity, betrayal and base human instincts marked all personal relations. Couched in a gritty and richly metaphorical spoken style, such novels, and their filmic counterparts, created an iconography of the city and a criminal underclass that resonated with the challenges of post-war European reconstruction.

As David Platten argues, this model, when transposed to France, shifted the narrative focus from the individual to the collective: 'Thus, in France the intrinsic fatalism of the *noir* concentrated in the individual protagonist is presented as a reflection and sometimes a consequence of wider, societal malaise.'[22] This is evident in the work of early French *roman noir* novelists who, even when their fictions are ostensibly located in American settings, mediate on contemporary French realities, such as the campaign to end the death penalty or anxiety over American economic investment in the form of the Marshall Plan.[23] For in France, the first exponents of the *roman noir* appropriated the form for a critique of recent French social and political histories. They produced popular narratives that spoke to readers' concerns and that were intended to energise them into considering the inequities of post-war reconstruction, particularly the human costs of rapid modernisation and economic expansion.

In terms of the war years themselves, the early French *roman noir* authors modelled them along three axes. Firstly, like their American counterparts, they proposed a vision of social fracture. The *roman noir* brought to the surface the transgressions and social disorder of living under the rule of Vichy and the German invader. French *roman noir* writers, such as Léo Malet, probed the gaping chasm between the claims of national resistance and the reality of defeat, occupation and liberation. In *Nestor Burma contre CQFD* (1945), for example, the war is not a neutral backdrop but a malign presence which cruelly ends the dreams of the narrator-detective, Nestor Burma, for a happy ending with the derailment of a train carrying his lover to safety. The deprivations and restrictions of living under occupation, such as rationing and territorial partition, and the sometimes dubious and illegal means required to make ends meet, such as the black market, are all present in Burma's adventures and are a catalyst for action. This is the case in Malet's first novel, *120, rue de la gare* (1942) which begins in a prisoner-of-war camp and takes Burma across occupied and unoccupied France in search of a treasure that reveals the extent of black market dealing, social inequality and the scope of money and privilege to grease the wheels of power. Early French *roman noir* novelists created a fictional universe in stark contrast to the Vichy-sponsored values of family, work and fatherland. They projected a vision of France given over to endemic corruption, hypocrisy and fear of the authorities, as in Malet's 1949 short story, 'Hélène en danger' where Burma's secretary and accomplice, Hélène, is denounced for resistance activism.

Secondly, the *roman noir* allowed French writers of these years to cast the war years in the poetics of urban dystopia. *Noir* aesthetics were exploited to depict a nation grappling with the moral dilemmas of occupation. The city as a place of violence and persecution, a country on the verge of collapse, a culture overwhelmed by rampant greed and self-interest, such *noir* features were an apposite screen on which to cast a France given over to total occupation and rule by a foreign power. Perhaps the most recurrent metaphor for such a vision of defeated France in these early fictions is the abandoned house. In *120 rue de la gare*, the crime scene for the graphic torture of a retreating soldier in June 1940 is a country house, revisited by the narrator-detective many months later and described as follows:

> Au milieu d'une minuscule clairière, une maison isolée nous apparut. Il se dégageait de cette demeure, assiégée pas les mauvaises herbes, une intolérable impression d'angoisse et de tristesse. La grande surface de la façade disparaissait sous le lierre et même, à l'étage, la végétation parasitaire obstruait une fenêtre. Les volets étaient clos. Les marches du perron étaient recouvertes, sous la neige, d'un tapis de feuilles pourries … A l'intérieur, une odeur nauséabonde de renfermé, de moisissure et d'abandon, nous accueillit.[24]

This pillaged and ravaged house can be read as symbolising the isolation of a nation which has submitted to the occupier and where nothing remains untouched, not even the private space of the home. The shuttered windows gesture at a collective lack of vision, an inability to see where and what to do next. Indeed the house, like many others in Malet's war fiction, is associated with suffering and is more of a tomb than a house, where death is arbitrary and ever-present.[25]

Lastly, the *roman noir* model offered French writers a cast of character types who could be quickly adapted to a French war context. Those selected were rarely in the mould of the wise-cracking private eye, such as Chandler's Philip Marlowe or Hammett's Sam Spade; Léo Malet's narrator-detective Nestor Burma is something of an exception in this respect. Rather, the character types that were transposed into early French crime fiction about the Second World War were the anti-heroes of the *roman noir* universe: the *femme fatale*, figure of feminine betrayal and submission, and the male victim, plagued by inner demons and subject to external pressures that threatened to destroy a fragile sense of self-belief. It is in this latter guise that the French resister is cast in the majority of early French *roman noir* of the immediate post-war years. The idealised male prototype of the resistance epic is absent and in his place is a protagonist who embodies an inflammatory vision of resistance in-fighting, amorality and marginalisation. By rejecting heroic models of masculine subjectivity, such popular crime fictions can be seen to engage with concerns that the voice of the individual resister was being edited out of the national picture in favour of a mythic narrative which falsified the profound moral and political divisions that had opened up under occupation.[26]

Strategies of contestation

Of the three authors under consideration here, two wrote with first-hand experience of resistance activism. According to biographical material produced to accompany a retrospective of his work in 2001,[27] André Héléna was a member of the Sournia *maquis* affiliated to the Brutus resistance network. Jean Meckert, later to gain critical recognition under the name Jean Amila, was active in the *maquis* in the Yonne region.[28] Gilles Morris also wrote from personal memories, having lived in Le Havre during the Allied bombing raids of the final months of the war and worked in a repatriation camp for GIs. He drew upon these experiences for his 1954 novel, *Assassin, mon frère*.[29] However, none of the three novelists chose to write about their wartime experiences in the form of a memoir or autobiography, adopting instead the fictionalising format of the *roman noir*. The value of their work does not reside, therefore, in a referential reading of resistance activism or liberation politics but rather in what these texts reveal about the attitudes and the values of the immediate post-war years. What they share is a deep distrust of narratives of resistance heroism and bravery. This is achieved in the literary template of *noir* by accentuating three aspects of the resistance record: the political factionalism of resistance, the violence and moral ambiguities of activism and, lastly, the post-war marginalisation of resisters. These three aspects offer an antagonistic vision of resistance and its legacies, filtered through the viewpoint of the male resister.

Firstly, all three authors project a vision of the internecine conflicts of the Resistance and the political factionalism of the early post-war years. *Nous avons les mains rouges* (1947), Jean Meckert's fourth novel, did not meet with commercial or critical success, a fact that Meckert would later attribute to its subject matter which he deemed to be 'too hard' for contemporary readers.[30] It would be republished in the early 1990s but would not stand as one of Meckert's most acclaimed works.[31] The narrative focuses on the figure of Laurent, a convicted murderer released from prison two years after the war's end. With no sense of political conviction, Laurent is recruited by chance to a renegade *maquis* group active in a mountainous region. This group is presented as an assortment of extreme left-wing activists who castigate the post-war purges for their leniency and have refused to accept the transition to democracy, interpreting the decision of the French Communist Party to join a government of national unity as a betrayal. Led by the charismatic d'Essartaut, the group engages in 'punishment missions' against known profiteers and collaborators who have escaped post-war sanction. Indeed, the group is represented as operating according to an anachronistic 'culture of the outlaw' that has exceeded its original purpose as a rallying point of opposition to Vichy and the Germans.[32] Resistance has now degenerated into a form of wholly unjustified insurrectional violence that one former supporter of the group likens to the abhorrent violence of its wartime fascist adversaries.[33]

At one level, the primacy of resistance as armed combat is reinforced in the epic tale of a band of brothers opposing an oppressive post-war order. Yet, such a formulation is turned on its head as Meckert presents the dogmatic sectarianism of the isolated group and their sacrifice of Laurent, politically untutored and expendable. He is murdered by another group member and his death is used to mask the group's involvement in the murder of two notorious wartime collaborators. While the novel may indeed be read as a demystification of the Resistance,[34] it is also productive to read its graphic and violent depiction of resistance as a comment upon the politics of liberation France. Its focus is not upon wartime resistance but upon the exploitation of a resistance legacy in the context of hardening Cold War relations and their impact on French domestic politics.[35]

From such a perspective, the death of the individual male resister, be-trayed from inside the group, undercuts the epic narrative of resistance self-sacrifice and highlights the sectarian uses of resistance in the flux of immediate post-war French (and global) politics.

In a similar vein, the individual resister's sacrifice for sectarian politi-cal purposes is evident in *Nous sommes tous des assassins*, a film directed by André Cayatte, and novelised by Meckert in 1952. The novel was re-published in 2008 in a major re-edition of Meckert's early work.[36] Film and novel are primarily concerned with the injustices of the continu-ing use of the death penalty in France and this is the major focus of the film. However, both novel and film ground their critique of the social and political inequalities of such a legalised practice in the politics of the war years and the manipulation of a young male resister by the higher echelons of the Resistance who do not want to dirty their hands with the bloody business of war. In the novel and film, René, an illiterate juvenile delinquent, is recruited into the Resistance following a chance encoun-ter with a printer, Sautier.[37] Narrated in flashback from René's cell at the liberation, the film and novel present this male resister as an uncom-prehending pawn in the internal power politics of the Resistance; he is manipulated into murdering Sautier whose anarchist sympathies rub up against the post-war aspirations of his Gaullist superiors. As novel and film reach their bleak ending, René comes to a belated realisation of the flawed nature of a generation of father figures, both individual (Sautier) and collective (the resistance network), and of the personal and politi-cal capital to be accrued from the myth of the Resistance. Confronting Mme Sautier with his part in the death of her husband, René notes ironi-cally that she prefers the war story of her husband's glorious death at the hands of German soldiers to that of execution by one of his resistance colleagues: 'Je la comprends, la pauvre Francine, elle préfère être veuve d'un héros, plutôt que d'un traître'.[38] In this fictional universe, everyone is complicit in endorsing a resistance epic that glorifies rather than reveal-ing uncomfortable home truths. The narrative highlights the hypocrisies of a ruling class who claim to represent moral authority but, as their dis-regard for René demonstrates, are prepared to use the cover of clandes-tine operations to further a post-war political agenda.

Secondly, these French *roman noir* of the 1940s and 1950s represent the Resistance as marked by the violence and moral ambiguities of its times. This representation of resistance is gleefully portrayed in André Héléna's diptych, *Les Salauds ont la vie dure!* (1949) and *Le Festival des macchabées* (1951). Héléna courted controversy with his incendiary depiction of the war years. *Les Salauds ont la vie dure!* was condemned as an affront to public decency in 1953 and the film adaptation, already in production, was axed due to government pressure.[39] However, the novels were republished in the early 1950s and 1960s and have since been re-published in the 1980s and 2000s, indicating their appeal as antagonistic cultural narratives of the Second World War.[40] The main protagonist and narrative viewpoint in both novels is Maurice Delbar, a Parisian gangster, whose picaresque journeys across occupied France trace the violent and unpredictable story of an occasional resister. Alternately a *maquis* fighter, a paid assassin for an American intelligence network and a rogue agent, Delbar is the embodiment of David Platten's observation that 'in these extraordinary times it is no longer the criminal who needs to adapt, but the law-abiding citizen who must adapt to the code of the underworld'.[41] As Maurice himself notes, the skills of subterfuge, deceit, disguise, dar-ing and a flagrant disregard for moral standards make him an excellent operative for any side in the war: 'Maurice Delbar, un peu agent secret, un peu truand. Un mec sans beaucoup de scruples et qui avait, on ne sait pourquoi, le don de se fourrer dans les situations telles qu'il en avait per-du tous ses scruples, petit à petit. Le genre de mec qui ne s'adapte qu'aux périodes exceptionnelles.'[42] Indeed, it is this presentation of resistance as adaptation to the moral turpitude of occupation that marks Héléna's work. Successful resistance is acceptance of the law of the jungle, match-ing violence with violence and putting self-interest before any abstract notion of collective good.

Yet Héléna highlights the personal costs of this seemingly cavalier atti-tude to life under occupation. Maurice is dogged by his past and haunted by the spectre of his one-time lover, Hermine, the first casualty of his murderous spree. While he may emerge triumphant at the Liberation, a pervasive sense of doom and fatalistic despair casts a sombre light on the dark years. This is reflected, as with the wartime fiction of Malet, in the disused buildings and urban squalor which are a constant feature of his novels. These symbolise the decline of France and the deleterious state not only of its infrastructure but also of its belief systems, values and hopes under occupation. Indeed, the sole concerns of those whom Delbar meets seem to be their material well-being: 'leurs petites histoires sordides de pantoufles, de charbon et de ravitaillement'.[43] There is no place here for high-flown ideals or political aspirations. The war years may have offered opportunities for violent self-indulgence but, the nov-els suggest, the legacies of the war years are not the glories of resistance, rather personal suffering, loss and social marginalisation.

Lastly, to varying degrees, the French *roman noir* of the late 1940s and 1950s depicts the marginalisation of the individual resister, upsetting any notion that he might offer a moral or political compass for postwar French society. This representation of the Resistance is portrayed in Gilles Morris's *Assassin, mon frère* (1954), which won the prestigious Grand prix de littérature policière in 1955. It has since been republished three times and Morris himself, in the preface to the 1990 edition, has described his novel as a 'polar-document', emphasising the novel's basis in the author's first-hand experiences of the liberation period.[44] The novel is set in the Philip Morris American repatriation camp in Le Havre in 1945. This was one of the 'cigarette' camps, staging areas for GIs going to the front at the time of the D-Day landings and then returning home. The action of the novel focuses on a group of former *maquis* resisters who work as telegram operators sending messages to American families back home awaiting the return of the GIs. Well-paid though their position is, they, and every other employee in the camp, are involved in black market trafficking: from the Red Cross volunteers to the German prisoners of war who work in the kitchens. Indeed, the camp comes to symbolise a whole series of clandestine transactions, both financial and sexual, in which European characters are presented as parasites on a largely beneficent American economy. In this *noir* fictional universe, liberation France functions as a nation that, having prostituted itself to one occupying power, is now beholden, in different circumstances, to another. The American characters are presented throughout as infantilised objects of derision for the French characters who perceive them to be insensitive and uncomprehending of the horrors recently experienced by occupied Europe.

The crime intrigue of the novel concerns the death of Raoul Milaud, a former *maquis* fighter, found killed on foreign soil: as he is murdered within the American camp the case falls under American jurisdiction. The murder weapon, a piece of shrapnel from an American bomb dropped on Le Havre during the final months of the war, represents the moral ambivalences of war. For, if the Americans are positioned as the victors, they are also depicted as creating enormous civilian suffering. This is writ large on the city of Le Havre presented as one vast necropolis, its citizens dispossessed and its urban infrastructure destroyed: 'Le cadavre d'une ville qu'ils avaient connue vivante, ardente … le théâtre municipal effondré, engloutissant dans ses caves plus de 200 victimes … le tunnel des tramways dans lequels plusieurs centaines de personnes étaient mortes, emmurées, lentement, cruellement, parmi les hocquets d'asphyxie et la lutte aveugle des survivants'.[45] The murder of Milaud, committed in the shower block of the camp under cover of darkness, reinforces further the sense of national indignity and the inability of resisters and the Resistance to represent a force for moral good.

It falls to the main protagonist, Milaud's *maquis* colleague, Robert Dévécoze to identify the culprit and to exact a form of justice. Yet Dévécoze's investigation uncovers further layers of French moral and political subjugation. For if the spectre of civil war does not enter the text directly at the level of exegesis, the eventual resolution of the crime relies upon a network of metaphors that highlight internecine conflict. Duplicity and betrayal permeate all social relations, as Dévécoze discovers in his attempts to assess individual character motives and opportunities for murder. Those he wishes to blame, such as the American GIs, prove ultimately to be blameless. The murderer is much closer to home and is revealed to be one of the *maquis* band of brothers who has killed Milaud for perhaps the most clichéd of reasons, sexual jealousy. From victim to detective and murderer, the legacy of resistance is continually redefined in the novel. Indeed, Dévécoze's own form of retribution, executing the murderer with his own weapon, the American shrapnel, undermines any suggestion of the resister (or the Resistance) as the moral arbiter of justice or authority. In this fictional universe, *noir* stands for crimes of war that continue to circulate, like a contagion, infecting the fabric of French society and disrupting any attempt to find solace in an epic narrative of resistance.

Conclusion

As discussion of these five novels has demonstrated, the late 1940s and the early 1950s in France were neither a time of blanket glorification of resistance nor silence and denial of its excesses and moral ambiguities. French crime fictions were part of a circuit of texts which challenged official preferences for stories of honour over tragedy, sacrifice over loss and justice over retribution. From the representation of sectarian political conflicts in Meckert's work to the amorality and violence of Héléna's fiction and the marginalisation of Morris's resisters in war-torn Le Havre, these novels set out a counter-history of resistance in which fictionalised male resisters undermine the national epic, so prevalent in France of the period. The charge of such antagonistic depictions owes much to the cultural politics of *noir* fiction, with its privileging of a doomed anti-hero and a dystopian social vision. When grafted onto war fiction, the *roman noir* also illuminates the internal contradictions and moral ambiguities of the resistance epic in three important respects.

Firstly, these crime fictions confirm Henry Rousso's thesis that, in the early years of France's Vichy syndrome (1944–54), there was a profound division between the Resistance as founding myth and the contingent and random trajectories of individual resisters: 'dans ces années-là a pris corps l'une des tensions majeures du syndrome, qui fait de la Résistance un mythe fondateur et des résistants des individus encombrants'.[46] Such a mismatch between legend and lived experiences provides the critical and creative momentum for these popular fictions. Male protagonists are excluded from the body politic even as they undertake illegal acts in its name, such as the narrator-protagonist René in *Nous sommes tous des assassins*, or they are sacrificed for a dubious greater good, such as the resister-convict Laurent in *Nous avons les mains rouges*.[47] Existential influences are discernible in such fictions as the main protagonists live with the remorselessness of guilt and the burden of their responsibility towards others, brother-in-arms as well as enemies and victims of their wartime actions. Indeed, the focus on the conflicted male resister in such fictions, the *frère-ennemi*, may be explained by reference to the broader post-war intellectual context in which questions of individual agency and resistance legacy were keenly debated. As Roderick Kedward notes in his reading of resistance narratives in 1950s France, this 're-rooting of resistance', away from the dominant political narratives of Gaullism and communism towards individual choice, may have contributed to the fracturing of a resistance legacy in the 1950s. However, it also reinforced a set of humanist principles and values that would be remobilised in later decades in relation to the anti-torture campaign during the Algerian War.[48]

Secondly, these crime fictions demonstrate the weight of past-present relations already at work in the evolution of memories of the Second World War. Even as wartime sits within the lifespan and experiences of the authors, these fictionalised reconstructions of resistance are inflected by the fears and concerns of the late 1940s and the early 1950s. The hardening of the Cold War and its political divisions is evident in Meckert's *Nous avons les mains rouges* in a narrative that condemns the factionalism of left-wing politics and the excesses of doctrinaire communism. From the opposite end of the political spectrum, Morris's *Assassin, mon frère* launches a vehement attack on the *coca-colonisation* of France and the corrosive effects of American-style consumerism.[49] In the novel, France is portrayed as caught between attraction and repulsion for an ally whose war record encompasses both the destruction and liberation of Le Havre. Such crime fictions highlight how, throughout the post-war period, memories of the Second World War would be reconstructed through the prism of the present.

Finally, these early French *roman noir* reveal the longevity of antagonistic narratives of the Resistance in French literary production. While such strategies of contestation have been commented upon in the work of younger generations of writers, such as Didier Daeninckx,[50] these early crime novels assert the persistence of contestation and critique from the late 1940s. Indeed the critical and commercial rediscovery of Meckert and Héléna in recent decades (including republication in the 2000s) may suggest that, after decades of relative obscurity, their disabused portraits of war have now found a more receptive readership, one that testifies to a pronounced cultural shift in French war memories.[51] From an era which tended to valorise the military prowess of heroes, we have now entered a period where the unjust suffering of innocent victims has captured the public imagination. The human, non-heroic mode of these crime fictions speaks to such a sensibility and can be read in parallel with depictions of resistance in films of the 2000s, such as Robert Guédiguian's *L'Armée du crime* (2009) and its focus on the decimation of the Main d'Oeuvre Immigrée resistance group via the figure of Armenian poet and resister, Missak Manouchian, or *Les Hommes libres* (2010), directed by Ismaël Ferroukhi, which examines the lives of Algerian resisters in occupied Paris.[52] However, this is not to detract from the significance of these crime fictions at their point of production. In their recasting of resistance via the individual, such novels offer a different narrative patterning of war memories to an epic tale of resistance. They provide textual evidence of the extent to which the resistance epic, even at its inception, was built upon a cluster of other representations, ones which would gain greater cultural currency later on.

Notes

1 Charles de Gaulle, *Discours et messages I* (Paris: Plon, 1970), pp. 439–40 (Paris! Paris violated! Paris broken! Paris martyred! But Paris liberated! Liberated by its own efforts, liberated by its people with the help of the armies of France, with the support and help of the whole of France, of fighting France, of the one true France, of eternal France).

2 Pieter Lagrou, *The Legacy of Nazi Occupation: Patriotic Memory and National*

Recovery in Western Europe, 1945–1965 (Cambridge: Cambridge University Press, 2000), p. 2.

3   The French Resistance, as a war story of victory against overwhelming odds, has come to stand as an enduring legacy of the Second World War for France. The continuing power of such a war story was illustrated in June 2010 during the celebrations to mark the seventieth anniversary of Charles de Gaulle's 18 June 1940 call to the French nation to carry on the struggle against the German invader. Media coverage of President Sarkozy in London, united with British Prime Minister David Cameron, offered the most recent public expression of the epic narrative that the Resistance has bequeathed France.

4   In the early post-war years, a story circulated that Eisenhower had credited the French Resistance with providing support at the Liberation equivalent to fifteen Allied divisions. Cited in Henri Michel, *Histoire de la Résistance en France (1940–1944)* (Paris: Presses Universitaires de France, 1950), p. 118.

5   Michel, *Histoire de la Résistance en France*, p. 125 (constitutes one of the most magnificent episodes in French history).

6   Lagrou, *The Legacy of Nazi Occupation*, p. 39, supports such a claim with the following figures: of the 1,036 awards, 783 went to members of the Free French, 107 to intelligence agents and only 157 to members of the internal resistance (some nominees fell into more than one category). Indeed, the self-promotion and outright careerism of some of these nominations is bitterly commented upon in a number of crime fictions from this period, see André Héléna, *Le Festival des macchabées* (Paris: Editions E-Dite, 2001), p. 282.

7   See Nathan Bracher's analysis of the Mont Valérien site as Gaullist epic and its re-appropriation in the work of contemporary sculptor and documentary filmmaker Pascal Convert in, 'Remembering the French resistance: ethics and poetics of the epic', *History and Memory*, 19:1 (2007), 39–67.

8   Simon Kitson, 'Creating a "nation of resisters"? improving French self-image, 1944–6', in Monica Riera and Gavin Schaffer (eds), *The Lasting War: Society and Identity in Britain, France and Germany after 1945* (Basingstoke: Palgrave Macmillan, 2008), pp. 67–85 (p. 71).

9   See Michel, 'Le martyre de la résistance' in *Histoire de la Résistance en France*, pp. 119–24.

10 Luc Capdevila, 'Le mythe du guerrier et la construction sociale d'un éternel masculin après la guerre', *Revue française de psychanalyse*, 62:2 (1998), 607–723.

11 See Fabrice Virgili, *Shorn Women: Gender and Punishment in Liberation France* (Oxford: Berg, 2002).

12 Pierre Nora, 'Mi-vainqueur, mi-vaincu', in Anne Simonin and Hélène Clastres (eds), *Les Idées en France (1945–1988): une chronologie* (Paris: Gallimard-Le Débat, 1989), pp. 27–33.

13   Nora, 'Mi-vainqueur, mi-vaincu', p. 29 (a familial and ideological settling of scores).

14   The French communist party (PCF) claimed the title of *le parti des 75,000 fusillés* (the party of the 75,000 martyrs) in homage to those of its members purported to have died in the battles against fascist Germany and its allies. Both the PCF and the Gaullists agreed that the nation as a whole had resisted, but differed on who had led the Resistance. A pro-Vichy war narrative highlighted the excesses of the Liberation: arbitrary violence, summary executions and a partisan process of post-war purges.

15   Lagrou, *The Legacy of Nazi Occupation*, p. 297.

16   See Annette Wieviorka, *Déportation et génocide: entre la mémoire et l'oubli* (Paris: Editions Plon, 1992) for a discussion of responses to the early testimonies of Jewish survivors in France.

17   See Susan Suleiman, 'Memory troubles: remembering the occupation in Simone de Beauvoir's *Les Mandarins*', *French Politics, Culture and Society*, 28:2 (2010), 4–17.

18   Margaret Atack, 'Representing the occupation in the novel of the 1950s: ne jugez pas', *Cincinnati Romance Review*, 29 (Fall 2010), 76–88 (76).

19   For a study of the relationship between French and American *roman* and *film noir* over the post-war period, see Alistair Rolls and Deborah Walker, *French and American Noir: Dark Crossings* (Basingstoke: Palgrave Macmillan, 2010).

20   See Claire Gorrara, 'Post-war French crime fiction: the advent of the *roman noir*', in Claire Gorrara (ed.), *French Crime Fiction* (Cardiff: University of Wales Press, 2009), pp. 51–70, for the debates surrounding the arrival of hard-boiled crime fiction in post-war France.

21   Raymond Chandler, 'The simple art of murder', reproduced in *Pearls are a Nuisance* (Harmondsworth: Penguin Books, 1966), pp. 181–99 (p. 194).

22   David Platten, *The Pleasures of Crime: Readings in Modern French Crime Fiction* (Amsterdam: Rodopi-Chiasma, 2011), pp. 69–70.

23   See Claire Gorrara, 'Cultural intersections: the American hard-boiled detective novel and early French *roman noir*', *Modern Language Review*, 98:3 (2003), 590–601, for a discussion of two early French *roman noir* novelists and their use of the genre for social critique and commentary.

24   Léo Malet, *120, rue de la gare* (Paris: Editions 10/18, 1983), p. 143. 'We came to a house standing alone in a little clearing. Weeds were closing in all round it, and it gave off a terrible aura of suffering and sadness. Most of the front of the house was overgrown with ivy, which completely obscured one of the first-floor windows. The shutters were closed, and a carpet of leaves showed through the snow on the steps. ... Inside the house we were met with a sickening smell of mildew and decay', Léo Malet, *120, rue de la gare*, trans. Peter Hudson (London: Pan Books, 1991), pp. 131–2.

25   I am grateful to Keir Waddington for his observation that the abandoned

house can be read as a transhistorical metaphor of wartime loss and civilian suffering. In a French literary frame, its use is evident in a range of war fiction particularly relating to the Franco-Prussian war. See, for example, Maupassant's short story 'La Mère Sauvage' (1884) and Zola's *La Débâcle* (1892).

26   A sense of betrayal at the political recasting of resistance in the immediate post-war era is evident in Jean Cassou's *La Mémoire courte* (1953). In this short polemical essay, Cassou, a former resister, berates France for failing to take responsibility for its Vichy past and for sacrificing the spiritual legacy of resistance in pursuit of a morally compromised national reconciliation.

27   This retrospective took place at the Bibliothèque des littératures policières (Bilipo), Paris, 11 May–31 August 2001.

28   See Jérôme Garcin, 'Jean Meckert, toujours vert!', *L'Evénement du jeudi* (21–27 July 1994), pp. 84–7, for an overview of Meckert's career.

29   See his autobiography for further details of his wartime itinerary: Gilles Morris-Dumoulin, *Le Forçat de l'Underwood* (Paris: Manya, 1993).

30   'Entretiens avec Jean Meckert/Amila', *Polar*, 16 (1995), 32–79 (41). It was, however, adapted as a theatre play in 1950 so demonstrating Meckert's personal commitment to the subject matter.

31   Jean Meckert, *Nous avons les mains rouges* (Paris: Gallimard, 1947); second edition, Meckert, *Nous avons les mains rouges* (Paris: Encrage, 1993). The latter edition has a postscript by Didier Daeninckx.

32   Meckert's representation of resistance resonates with Roderick Kedward's analysis of the *maquis* as offering 'a structural alternative to Vichy legality, a veritable culture of the outlaw'. See Roderick Kedward, 'The maquis and the culture of the outlaw (with particular reference to the Cevennes)', in Roderick Kedward and Roger Austin (eds), *Vichy France and the Resistance: Culture and Ideology* (London: Croom Helm, 1985), pp. 232–51 (p. 245).

33   Meckert, *Nous avons les mains rouges* (Paris: Gallimard, 1947), p. 118.

34   Jean-Pierre Deloux, 'Blanche à filet rouges', *Polar*, 16 (1995), 2–31 (9).

35   For this reading of the novel, see Didier Daeninckx, 'Jean Amila, l'inconnu du noir-express', *La Mémoire longue*, p. 285.

36   Jean Meckert, *Nous sommes tous des assassins* (Paris: Editions Joëlle Losfeld, 2008).

37   This representation of wartime activism as a personal whim would receive greater exposure in the 1970s and the *mode rétro* in films, such as Louis Malle's *Lacombe Lucien* (1974).

38   Meckert, *Nous sommes tous des assassins*, p. 231 (I can understand poor Francine, she prefers to be the widow of a hero, rather than a traitor).

39   Robert Deleuse, 'Petite histoire du roman noir français', *Les Temps modernes*, 595 (1997), 53–87 (63).

40   André Héléna, *Les Salauds ont la vie dure!* (Paris: Editions World Press, 1949). Subsequent editions are: Paris: Editions Le Trotteur, 1953; Paris: U.G.E 1986; Paris: Editions E-Dite, 2001. André Héléna, *Le Festival des*

macchabées (Paris: A. Fleury, 1951). Subsequent editions: Paris: S.E.P.F.E. 1960; Paris: U.G.E,1986; Paris: Editions E-Dite, 2001.

41   Platten, *The Pleasures of Crime*, p. 81.

42   Héléna, *Le Festival des macchabées*, p. 254 (Maurice Delbar, part secret agent, part crook. A guy without many scruples and who had, for some reason, a real gift for getting mixed up in bad situations so that , little by little, he lost what scruples he had. The kind of guy who is best suited to such exceptional times).

43   Héléna, *Le Festival des macchabées*, p. 52 (their sordid little stories of slippers, coal and food rations).

44   Gilles Morris, *Assassin, mon frère* (Monaco: Editions du Rocher, 1990), p. 10. Other editions of the novel are: Paris: Presses de la Cité 1954; Geneva: Edito-service, 1983; Paris: Fleuve noir, 1983.

45   Gilles Morris, *Assassin, mon frère* (Paris: Presses de la Cité, 1954), p. 153 (the corpse of a city that they had known passionately alive … the municipal theatre collapsed, burying 200 people in its cellars … the tramway tunnel in which several hundred people had died, walled in, cruelly, slowly, suffocating and the blind struggle of the survivors).

46   Henry Rousso, *Le Syndrome de Vichy de 1944 à nos jours* (Paris: Editions du Seuil, 1990), pp. 75–6 (in these years, one of the major tensions of the syndrome took shape, between the Resistance as founding myth and resisters as troublesome individuals).

47   In reading these novels, I would tend to reject the view that these writers are somehow anti-resistance or complicit with right-wing attacks on the Resistance which emphasised the brutality and bloodshed of the liberation period. It is the manipulation of the post-war legacy which is criticised not the resistance activism of the few.

48   Roderick Kedward, 'Re-rooting the resistance in post-war France' in *The Lost Decade: the 1950s in European History, Politics, Society and Culture*, eds. Heiko Feldner, Claire Gorrara and Kevin Passmore (Cambridge: Cambridge Scholars Press, 2011), pp. 60–74.

49   For French *roman noir* that provide a transposed critique of American-identified values and cultural mores, see Terry Stewart, *La Belle Vie* (1950) and John Amila [Jean Meckert], *'Y a pas de bon dieu!* (1950).

50   See, for example, his *La Mort n'oublie personne* (Paris: Gallimard, 1989) which focuses on the account-settling of the immediate post-war years and the persecution of a genuine resister.

51   The recuperation of Jean Meckert/Amila has been particularly marked and led to the publication of previously unknown work, notably *La Marche au canon* (Paris: Editions Joëlle Losfeld, 2005), an account of a young French soldier's retreat during the defeat of France in May–June 1940. This is a fragment of a larger project devoted to the war years that was never completed.

52   See too Didier Daeninckx, *Missak* (Paris: Perrin, 2009) which revolves
      around the wartime activities of Missak Manouchian. Daeninckx's novel,
      set in 1955, deconstructs some of the more mythic aspects of Manouchian's
      posthumous reputation and investigates the communist appropriation of
      his legacy in the 1950s. Instead, it sets out the non-conformist resistance
      histories that such an appropriation has obscured.

2

Forgotten crimes: representing Jewish wartime experience in French crime fiction of the 1950s and 1960s

The 1950s and early 1960s in France have been discussed as years given over to a repression of the multiple histories and memories of the occupation. In her study of crises of memory and the Second World War, Susan Rubin Suleiman encapsulates these dominant perceptions when she refers to a 'forced amnesia', reinforced in the legal sphere by a series of amnesties which freed the majority of French men and women who had been tried and convicted of crimes of collaboration.[1] Yet, as Suleiman notes, the legal application of amnesty rarely equates to a coming to terms with the past. Indeed, the very opposite may occur, as in the case of France, when the amnesties of the late 1940s and early 1950s inhibited public discussion of such crimes, shutting down the archives and the nascent process of historical investigation. For Suleiman, the 1950s can, therefore, be more properly analysed as a period which 'prevented a genuine working through of a painful history. Instead, they prescribed forgetting, turning the page on the past …'.[2]

This chapter will explore representations of Jewish wartime persecution and deportation in novels by Léo Malet and Hubert Monteilhet of the late 1950s and early 1960s. It will argue that the revelation of crimes against the Jewish community activates complex processes of disclosure, displacement and disavowal that can be read as a reflection upon broader configurations of French wartime guilt and complicity. The chapter will begin by outlining the social and cultural contexts for remembering the Second World War in France in the late 1950s and early 1960s. It will discuss some of the reasons for the muted recognition of Jewish wartime experiences. It will then focus on representations of Jewish communities under occupation in French crime fiction, before examining three novels by Malet and Monteilhet and the narrative strategies they deploy for exploring questions of individual and collective guilt and responsibility. In the fiction of both authors, subtle patterns of recognition and denial of anti-Semitic persecution are embedded in the crime intrigue, providing rich material for speculation on French wartime memory at a time of apparent forgetting.

Forgetting and remembering

During the 1950s and 1960s in France, official war stories coalesced on a Gaullist narrative of resistance, a resistance epic, as discussed in Chapter 1. Such an integrative myth was consolidated during the national com-memorations that accompanied the transfer of Jean Moulin's ashes to the Pantheon in December 1964. Moulin, de Gaulle's envoy to the internal resistance, had been tortured and murdered by his German captors in 1943 and had become a symbol of the resolve and sacrifice of the Resist-ance. For Henry Rousso, this meticulously planned spectacle was a po-litical act that marked de Gaulle's careful exorcism of earlier internecine disputes over the legacy of the Resistance and gave the public seal of approval to an abstracted image of an honourable resistance that drew all to it.[3] Yet, dominant war stories are formed by their interaction with other narratives of war and mutate in response to domestic and interna-tional developments.[4] With the transition from the Fourth to the Fifth Republic in France came both a consolidation of the resistance epic, as well as vocal challenges to its hegemony. The ferocity of France's wars of decolonisation, particularly in Algeria, had a considerable impact on representations of the war years, framing them in charged contexts that reactivated debate but in new and unexpected ways.[5] It is these years of transition, 1958–61, that critics have re-examined as a period when more nuanced representations of the war years gained greater prominence.[6] These probed controversial aspects of France's war record, such as the phenomenon of collaboration or the compromises of everyday survival in 'images of a France at war with itself'.[7] Amongst the alternate war sto-ries that can be traced in these transitional years are narratives of Jewish persecution and deportation.

A number of historians of the Second World War have commented upon the muted reception that greeted Jewish testimony of life in the concentration camps in immediate post-war France. As Pieter Lagrou notes, during the 1950s and 1960s: 'the awareness, the *prise de conscience*, of the specificity of the Jewish experience in the universe of Nazi persecu-tion had not permeated public opinion and that in reactions towards the survivors of genocide open hostility often prevailed'.[8] Lagrou grapples sensitively with the reasons for such marginalisation. These encompass the side-lining of Jewish war experiences due to post-war anti-Semitism which propagated images of Jewish treason and the lack of a Jewish resistance. He also examines the prevalence of an anti-fascist discourse that grouped Jews with other victims of Nazi persecution. Lastly, he points to the impact of a dominant patriotic memory in France, that of the resistance epic, that metaphorically hid Jewish survivors from view. In her study of the early accounts by French-Jewish survivors of the extermination camps, Annette Wieviorka comes to similar conclusions, pointing to the reluctance of survivors and their families to identify with the Jewish specificity of genocide.[9] She ascribes their attitudes to a belated and incomplete understanding of events, as well as to a desire to reintegrate into French Republican society. Many also chose to set aside self-identification as Jewish because it was an identity that had been perceived and lived as an imposition by the perpetrator.

Despite these observations on the marginality of public and personal acknowledgement of the specificity of the Holocaust in France, narratives of Jewish persecution, deportation and extermination are evident in the cultural production of the late 1950s and early 1960s. These are visible both in terms of direct portrayal and in more subtle and allusive ways, what Leah D. Hewitt calls the 'haunting presence' of the Jewish experience of the war years.[10] Indeed, as Joan B. Wolf has argued, since the French Revolution, Jews in France have functioned as 'something of a discursive screen onto which competing political projects could be projected', above all in relation to questions of national identity.[11] It is this discursive screen of Jewish experience and French national identity that will be investigated in novels by French crime novelists Léo Malet and Hubert Monteilhet via analysis of the tropes of disclosure, displacement and disavowal. For, as this chapter will argue, representations of crimes against Jewish characters in these popular fictions reveal both the legacies of Jewish wartime persecution and the tensions within French national memories during this transitional period.

Disclosure and displacement

In her study of the image of the Jew in French crime fiction, Nadine Rozenberg Akoun is drawn to the repeated evocation of the occupation and the Holocaust.[12] In the eighty-three *roman policier* which she examines between 1945 and 2001, thirty-five address the topic of the Second World War and its murderous toll on the Jewish population. Rozenberg Akoun argues that there is no sudden explosion of crime novels featuring the Holocaust in recent decades, as might be expected, but rather a continuous reflection on the experience of Jews in wartime France. Novels featuring the treatment of Jewish protagonists are equally distributed between 1945 and 1970 and 1970 to 2001. However, Rozenberg Akoun points to a shift in representation as partial recognition of Jewish persecution in the 1950s is transformed into polemical denunciation of anti-Semitism and French state collusion in the Holocaust in the 1980s and 1990s. For Rozenberg Akoun, the late 1940s and 1950s represent years when patterns of recognition and denial were rooted in the French cultural imaginary but which would be radically revisited decades later.

In her survey of French crime fiction from these early decades, Rozenberg Akoun focuses on writers such as André Héléna, whose work, while acknowledging the fear, flight and persecution of Jews in France, continues to reinforce images of Jewish villainy and victimisation.[13] This is evident in *Les Clients du Central Hôtel* (1959), set at the Liberation in Perpignan and which follows the wartime trajectories of the transient population of the Central Hotel. All of the guests harbour wartime secrets, such as the British secret agent, Vandevelde; the Spanish Republican refugee, Ramon; and the German informer, 'Lily Marlène'. Blumenstein, the Jewish character, is presented in a sympathetic light as a man forced by circumstances to flee but who, in the pre-war period, had lived with no sense of his racial difference: 'Et il était juif. Cela ne l'avait pas empêché d'aller en classe avec les gosses de son quartier, d'apprendre rudiment à gagner son pain, de payer ses impôts comme tout le monde et de partir à la guerre, lorsque les autres étaient partis'.[14] Yet, despite this sensitive portrait of exile and displacement, the novel ends by reaffirming the perennial association of Jewishness with financial power as Blumenstein is presented as having become a wealthy man in the aftermath of war.

The novels of Léo Malet provide intriguing confirmation of the patterns of recognition and denial that Akoun notes in representations of the Jewish community and the occupation in the 1950s. Malet's series, *Les Nouveaux Mystères de Paris*, published between 1954 and 1959, is considered one of the most accomplished series of French crime writing on the city. Each of the series' fifteen novels is set in a different *arrondissement* with Malet using the city space as a canvas on which to depict multi-layered histories where past and present, private and public, intersect. City space is no mere backdrop for action but functions as an imaginative landscape onto which individual psychology and social history are projected. The history of the Second World War and the wars of decolonisation are a recurrent reference in the narratives as their legacies trigger crime and disorder. As Nadia Dhoukar notes in her introduction to a re-edition of Malet's writing: 'La Seconde Guerre mondiale ou la guerre d'Algérie laissent des séquelles dans les consciences des hommes comme dans leur cadre de vie …'[15] Two of Malet's *Les Nouveaux Mystères de Paris* novels revolve around the legacies of Jewish wartime experiences.

Du rébecca rue des Rosiers (1958) and *Des kilomètres de linceuls* (1955) centre on secret histories of wartime Jewish persecution. The novels were republished in the 1970s, 1980s, 1990s and 2000s, an indication of the commercial success of Malet's series and its depiction of post-war France.[16] Narrated from the first-person perspective of private detective Nestor Burma, the novels position Burma as an intermediary for the reader as he unravels war stories that reveal a dual dynamic of disclosure and displacement of Jewish wartime persecution. Each is set in a resonant Parisian location for a history of the Jewish community in France: in *Du rébecca rue des Rosiers*, the rue des Rosiers in the Marais district of the IV *arrondissement* and, in *Des kilomètres de linceuls*, the rue des Jeûneurs in the Sentier district of the II *arrondissement*.[17] In both novels, it is via Burma's equivocal narration, both sensitive to the horrors of wartime events but also tainted with anti-Semitic stereotypes, that the war story of Jewish persecution is disclosed and displaced onto a richly evoked city space.[18]

In *Du rébecca rue des Rosiers*, the crime intrigue is triggered by the discovery of a woman's body at the apartment of Fred Baget, an acquaintance of Burma's and a well-known artist. The picture is complicated by the Jewish identity of the woman, Rachel Blum, and the collaborationist past of her host Baget who is fearful that the murder and subsequent investigation will lessen his chances of being awarded the *Légion d'honneur* to which he aspires. The murder weapon, an SS dagger with the inscription 'my honour is my loyalty', raises the spectre of continuing French anti-Semitism. This is reinforced by the language and reductive racial stereotypes of the novel, such as the derogatory terms Baget uses to label Rachel Blum, the casual racism of the police and the repeated reference to secondary characters who demonstrate a supposedly Semitic physiognomy and vices.[19] Burma's murder investigation criss-crosses Paris and converges on the figure of Saul Bramovici, a Jewish collaborator and Gestapo informer who denounced fellow Jews for profit and self-advancement. He escaped at the Liberation and fled to London to run a crime syndicate and has now returned to Paris under an assumed identity and is hiding in the secret wartime refuge of a Jewish family.

As with many other Burma adventures, the search is for a criminal presence masked by another name and identity. Bramovici has assumed the heritage of a Jewish survivor of the concentration camps, Samuel Aaronovicz, deported with his family but who survived. He becomes yet another victim on Bramovici's quest to remain beyond the reach not only of the police but also a criminal gang, searching for hidden occupation gold, and an Israeli military commander, Moyes, who seeks revenge for those whom Bramovici betrayed to the Gestapo. The Jewish collaborator, Bramovici, masquerades, therefore, as a victim of the Holocaust adopting the identity of one of his own victims. Yet the character of the fictional Bramovici also hides reference to a real incarnation of the Jewish collaborator, Joseph Joanovici, whose personal history of collaboration, trial, imprisonment and exile would come to an end in 1965.[20] Hiding in the cellar where the real Aaronovicz family sought refuge during the war years before their denunciation, Bramovici functions as a composite figure of Jewish wartime persecution and profiteering.[21]

In *Du rébecca rue des Rosiers*, the evocation of two privileged city places complicates the ostensible anti-Semitic discourse of the novel. These locations function as displaced metaphors, 'haunting presences' of Jewish experience that highlight broader debates on French wartime guilt and responsibility. The first location is Bramovici's hiding place, a disused house which exudes an air of loss and desolation in the twilight rain: 'La maison en question est vraiment sinistre, vénéneuse au possible, surtout à cette heure crépusculaire et sous le méchant crachin qui tombe. Sa façade s'écaille ... Un des battants du monumental portail de bois est couvert d'affiches, la plupart en hébreu, et d'inscriptions à la craie. Sur l'autre, est fixé un avertissement émaillé: DANGER.'[22] The graffiti, the Hebrew inscriptions and the warnings of danger mark out the wartime heritage of the building, while the sealed windows can be read as indicating a refusal on the part of the local community to see or understand its past as a sanctuary for Jewish families. Inside the house, in a hidden second cellar, is the Aaronovicz's wartime refuge, a sanctuary not for Jews escaping German and Vichy detection but for Bramovici who evades his responsibility for wartime murder and collaboration. The hidden cellar can be read as symbolising suppressed Jewish wartime memories, buried within the national psyche under the official narrative of national resistance and valour. The dark, damp crypt, the final resting place of the ironically named journalist Jacques Ditvrai (literally 'speaks true'), is suggestive of a burial chamber. Due for demolition, the house captures the horror of the war years and the collective temptation to erase the Jewish memory it represents.

The second location is the memorial to the Jewish victims of the Holocaust situated on the rue Geoffroy-L'Asnier, a visible site of remembrance in sharp contrast to Bramovici's hiding place. It is here that Bramovici is stoned to death by Jewish families, his battered body left by the gates for the police to collect. The ritualistic nature of this punishment and its location at the Mémorial juif indicate a very different narrative of Jewish wartime experience, one that affirms a heroic war story of Jewish agency as a form of retribution is enacted. Malet's crime fiction gestures, therefore, at a double vision of Jewish wartime experience writ large on the urban fabric of Paris. While the dialogue, character portrayals and themes of betrayal, collaboration and murder tell a tale of Jewish victimisation and criminality, *Du rébecca rue des Rosiers* also taps into other war stories of Jewish experience circulating in France in the 1950s. These recast the tragedy of deportation and extermination as a staging point in the traumatic journey of becoming for a people and for its nation, Israel. Such a redemptive narrative is evident in Malet's novel where Jewish courage and heroism jostle with victimisation and perpetration.[23] In its evocation of the spaces and places of persecution and retribution, *Du rébecca rue des Rosiers* provides the reader with a fractured and contradictory vision of Jewish wartime experience and its reception in French society of these transitional years.

In *Des kilomètres de linceuls*, similarly conflicted patterns of crime, betrayal and retribution are associated with the Jewish community. The narrative is again centred on a war story of Jewish denunciation and deportation. In this crime intrigue, Burma is asked by Esther Lévyberg, a Jewish concentration camp survivor, to discover the whereabouts of her former lover, Georges Moreno. Disfigured by an accidental fire during her internment, Esther carries the visible scars of her wartime deportation. As Burma progresses with his investigations, he discovers that the catalyst for a brutal series of murders is a buried history of the occupation, above all Esther's own secret that she denounced her family (and herself) as Jews to the authorities in revenge for their opposition to her relationship with Moreno. Parallel to this wartime secret is that of gangster Henri Péronnet, now Gérard Bonfils, a collaborator and associate of the Gestapo, sent to the concentration camps where he saved the life of Esther's brother, René, and is now using René's prosperous post-war business as a front for a counterfeit ring. As with the character of Bramovici in *Du rébecca rue des Rosiers*, Malet's crime narrative locates guilt and responsibility for Jewish wartime persecutions squarely within the Jewish community itself, this time in the person of Esther Lévyberg. Her auto-denunciation perpetuates stereotypes of Jewish dissimulation and betrayal.

The portrayal of Esther is troubling in the text. Her pariah status, symbolised by her facial disfigurement, is reinforced by repeated references to her abnormal sexual proclivities and her hatred of her brother and what she perceives as her family's denial of her happiness. Her choice to adopt a Jewish name, Esther, and to reject her previous identity (and the one under which Burma knew her) as Alice, signals her decision to assume a Jewish identity and to refuse the erasure of cultural and racial difference: 'Esther, rectifia-t-elle sèchement, Alice c'est un nom goy. Esther, ça, c'est du juif, du solide. Je suis une affreuse et ignoble juive. Si je n'avais pas été juive, rien de ce qui m'est arrivé ne me serait arrivé.'[24] In contrast, René's political aspirations and commercial success are presented as rampant ambition, although, as ever in Malet's prose, the experience of the concentration camp world is evoked as a form of explanation, if not justification, for such actions. Indeed, the world of the concentration camps emerges in the narrative as an ever-present cultural reference point: 'il me faudrait me dépatouiller tout seul, et agir vite, avec des chances de réussir aussi maigres que si elles revenaient d'un camp de déportation, elles aussi'.[25] In this darkly humorous quotation from Burma, the skeletal survivors of the camps are indirectly referenced as one of the metaphorical legacies of the *univers concentrationnaire*.

To a lesser extent than in *Du rébecca rue des Rosiers*, Parisian city space is a screen onto which attitudes and perceptions of Jewish wartime experiences are displaced. Rather, it is the profession and naming of the Lévyberg family business which accentuates the complex history of assuming Jewish identity in the aftermath of war. Fabric manufacturers, the Lévyberg empire has been rebranded as Les Tissus Berglevy post-war, inverting the patronymic syllables (Lévyberg to Berglevy), with an accompanying loss of accent. This can be read from a number of perspectives. Is Malet suggesting a family desire to disassociate itself from its Jewish heritage? Here, the German-identified *berg* precedes Levy as if a perpetrator legacy remains dominant. Conversely, does such a reworking of the family name suggest the impossibility of ever leaving such a heritage aside, even as it is recast for business purposes? As Malet's narrator makes clear in the final lines of the text, the choice of family name and profession is an important one for an understanding of the circuits of Jewish identity in the text: 'Tissus Berglevy. Cotonnades. Soieries. Lainages. Toiles.

Des écrans de cinéma pour le rêve? Des draps de lit pour l'amour? Des linceuls, pas autre chose'.[26] If clothing manufacture is traditionally associated with the Jewish community of Paris, in this crime fiction such an association has multiple resonances. It is the cinema screen and the escapism of popular entertainment. It is the clean sheets of the bedroom and the metaphorical clean sheet of a new beginning for the post-war Jewish community. It is also the shroud, the cloth of mourning. As the perpetual memory of loss, it can be read here as a metaphor for the millions of Jews deported and exterminated during the Holocaust.

Disclosure and disavowal

Le Retour des cendres (1961), also published in the transition years of the late 1950s and early 1960s, marks a radical departure from the tropes and patterns of preceding crime fiction depicting Jewish wartime experiences. Indeed, for Nadine Rozenberg Akoun, Hubert Monteilhet's fictional evocation of the life of a returning Jewish deportee at the Liberation 'contredit l'hypothèse ... selon lequel la période de l'après-guerre, les trente glorieuses, avait été un temps de déni et d'oubli des tragédies de l'occupation'.[27] The novel was a commercial and critical success, translated into nine different languages and quickly adapted for the screen by J. Lee Thompson as *The Return of the Ashes* in 1965, starring Maximilian Schell and Samantha Eggar.[28] The novel has been republished five times, most recently in 2008.[29] As the dust jacket to its 1966 re-edition underscores, the novel was promoted by its publishers not only as a crime novel but also as a modern tragedy of Shakespearian proportions as love descends into horror and murder.[30] Centred on the figure of Elisabeth Wolf, *Le Retour des cendres* explores the post-war fate of a Jewish concentration camp survivor and her ultimately tragic attempts to reintegrate herself into her former life as a doctor, wife and mother. The narrative addresses complex issues, such as the construction and disclosure of a Jewish identity in the wake of genocide, the self-justifications of the perpetrator and the lack of integration and acknowledgement of survivors at the Liberation.

Monteilhet's text is presented to the reader in the form of a private diary, that of Elisabeth Wolf, which opens on 29 June 1945, the day of her return to France from an unnamed concentration camp, and ends on 29 October 1945, the day on which she is murdered. This private account is framed in the letter of an investigating judge who sends the diary to Elisabeth Wolf's daughter, Fabienne. This is a ploy to persuade her to confess to her part in her mother's murder by gassing in the family apartment. From reading her diary entries, it transpires that Elisabeth decided not to return immediately to her husband, Stan, and her adult daughter, Fabi, on her return in France. Instead, she sets out to recompose herself via medical treatment and cosmetic surgery in order to be able to integrate into her old life with as much dignity as possible. However, it is while undergoing such a positive transformative that she is contacted by Stan and Fabi who have spotted her in front of a department store and who, believing her to be a convincing lookalike, ask if she will impersonate Elisabeth whom they assume must be dead. The narrator, Elisabeth Wolf, is assured that she will be rewarded for her theatrical performance with a percentage of their inheritance.

From here, the diary charts the complex interplay of identity and counter-identity as Elisabeth, the returning deportee, impersonates herself in an attempt to win back her husband whom she believes would have been repulsed by her returning self. As the narrative progresses, Stan is revealed to be an uncaring husband who has used his wife as the financier of his career as an international chess champion and who is prepared to go to any lengths to secure material gain and advancement. The tone of the diary entries darkens as the narrator comes to realise that her wartime denunciation and deportation were not by chance but the result of betrayal by Stan. This, together with Stan's affair with Fabi, his stepdaughter, leads to Elisabeth's growing realisation that a return to Paris cannot be engineered that would allow for a normative model of family life to be recreated.

The textual construction of a Jewish identity is one area where Monteilhet's text reworks and complicates the rather Manichaean creations of Malet's *Les Nouveaux Mystères de Paris* novels. In *Le Retour des cendres*, Monteilhet projects a diffuse and nuanced sense of Jewish identity and culture which cannot be connected to a particular geographical location or narrative type. Indeed, as Bryan Cheyette has argued in relation to English literature, literary representations of Jewishness can be more usefully approached as fluid and protean rather than defined in relation to fixed images, myths and stereotypes.[31] For Cheyette, what he terms the 'race-thinking' of a text needs to be positioned within a broader set of belief systems and to be understood as projections of national identities that articulate shifting and historically contingent social and political relations. In *Le Retour des cendres*, 'race-thinking' about Jewish war experiences can be read within a similar optic, reflecting not only on the specificity of Jewish war experiences but also indicating something of

French collective responses to the legacies of war. For, in Elisabeth Wolf's diary, the extent to which individuals assume or disavow their Jewish identity correlates to their acceptance or rejection of wartime guilt and responsibility.

In the case of the narrator, Elisabeth Wolf, her Jewish identity is one which she is vaguely aware of pre-war and which does not impinge upon her consciousness. Her roles as doctor, wife and mother are more deeply embedded as forms of self-identification than a sense of belonging to a Jewish diaspora. However, with wartime persecution, there comes a reversal of identification. As Elisabeth, the narrator, notes in flashback, others' targeting of her as Jewish brings her to re-evaluate what it means to be Jewish. In a fraught wartime encounter with Stan prior to her de-nunciation and deportation, Elisabeth refutes that her growing self-defi-nition as Jewish is based on religious, racial or ethnic considerations. She claims rather an identification with 'une communauté de souffrance que le temps a cimenté.'[32] This communitarian identity is confirmed on her return when the narrator assumes her Jewish identity, defiantly asking her cosmetic surgeon to craft her a Jewish nose in place of the scarred and broken camp legacy: 'J'avais un peu oublié que je l'étais. On me l'a rappelé très durement. Je dois tenir compte de ce rappel.'[33] For Elisabeth Wolf, the narrator, this defiant assumption of her Jewish identity signals an acceptance of the past and a willingness to confront the consequences of wartime events.

In sharp contrast, Stanislas Pilgrin, her husband and the man who de-nounces her to the authorities, refutes his Jewish identity.[34] Stan refuses to accept the objective existence of a Jewish identity in terms reminiscent of Sartre's provocative analysis of *la question juive* in 1946: 'Le Juif, c'est une vue de l'esprit. On est israélite comme on est chrétien, on est juif comme on est français … C'est une affaire d'imagination.'[35] Stan presents Jewish identity as a construction of the anti-Semite who projects his own fears, negations and inadequacies onto the other. For Stan, to assume a Jewish identity where none exists is an illusory attempt to make sense of the senseless persecution of the Second World War: 'Je crois en effet que tu souffres pour rien, reconnut-il [Stan]. Je sais que c'est très dur de souf-frir ainsi, mais cela vaut mieux que de donner à ses ennuis un sens dis-cutable. C'est plus digne.'[36] But this disavowal of Jewish identity is highly personalised as, in the last pages of the text, Stan reveals himself to have Jewish parentage and to be living under an assumed name. Stan is so violently opposed to his Jewish heritage being revealed publicly that he threatens to kill Elisabeth, the narrator. In *Le Retour des cendres*, Jewish identity is, therefore, not 'une affaire d'imagination' but has textual effects in the presentation of Stan as the perpetrator of the central crime of the text: Elisabeth Wolf's denunciation.

Le Retour des cendres provides the reader with a rare manifestation of a perpetrator's tale in these early post-war decades. Stan's confession to his role in Elisabeth's arrest in the autumn of 1943 is revelatory of attitudes towards Jewish persecution and deportation that are patterned elsewhere in this chapter, above all the location of guilt within the Jewish community itself. What is striking, however, about *Le Retour des cendres* is the voice accorded the perpetrator and the rhetorical strategies Monteilhet employs to evoke Stan's guilt and responsibility. In a carefully woven tissue of self-justification, Stan, firstly, presents his actions as a case of forced participation, opting for the lesser of two evils in denouncing his wife to German soldiers rather than the criminal elements of the French police: 'J'ai pensé, d'autre part, qu'il était plus noble de confier ma femme à des soldats. Le crime laisse un goût d'autant moins amer que les complices honorables sont plus nombreux'.[37] French collaboration is portrayed here not as ideologically driven but rather the result of greed and self-interest in sharp contrast to the 'complices honorables' of the German authorities. Secondly, Stan presents his denunciation as an act undertaken in ignorance of historical realities, above all the horrors of the concentration camps: 'il n'était pas facile, à l'époque, d'imaginer ce que pouvait bien être un camp de concentration dans un pays de dictature'.[38] Indeed, Monteilhet produces a set of 'exculpatory tales'[39] that resonate with Tzvetan Todorov's later investigation of the moral life of those who policed the concentration camps.[40] In terms of the narrative economy of *Le Retour des cendres*, this disavowal of culpability (forced participation and ignorance) intersects with a disavowal of Jewish identity. The inference of the text is, therefore, that a refusal to accept the existence and specificity of Jewish identity precludes the airing of broader questions of guilt, complicity and responsibility.

Lastly, *Le Retour des cendres* is a crime fiction about the impossibility of return. The Liberation is not lived as joyous celebration but rather as 'a moment of discovery of horror, or the start of mourning or … as an explosion of revenge'.[41] While Elisabeth Wolf may have physically returned from the camps, she is assailed by flashbacks to her deportation in the form of sensory memories that indicate her continuing entrapment in the past. Even the manner of her death, gassed in her family apartment, underscores the fact that her return to Paris is but a deferral of the fate that befell many of her fellow deportees. As the title of the book suggests, only the ashes of Elisabeth Wolf return or perhaps her return is from a place of ashes and death which she can never escape. In either case, the four months of her post-war life in Paris are the end point of a slow process of destruction begun elsewhere. Her desensitised response to the death of a young child in the opening sections of the diary dramatises yet further how removed she is from the moral norms of post-war life.[42] Indeed, the notion of the return itself is problematic within the exegesis of the novel. Attempted returns range from the re-enactment of her return at the Gare de l'Est for the purposes of establishing her fake identity as Elisabeth Wolf, to epistolary accounts designed to take revenge on Stan and Fabi, to imagined encounters between her real and impersonated self. None of these actual or fantasised occasions emerges to stand as the definite point of return. In its interplay of identities and allegiances, this fictional diary embodies the figurative impossibility for Elisabeth Wolf, the narrator, ever to return to French society.

Conclusion

In conclusion, the crime fictions discussed in this chapter demonstrate popular culture's engagement with narratives of Jewish wartime experience in the 1950s and 1960s. The conventions of crime fiction allow a secret history of Jewish persecution to emerge and for questions of guilt, responsibility and retribution to be aired. What characterises all of the novels discussed here is the traumatic process of disclosing wartime crimes against Jewish characters and the fatal consequences this has for individuals, families and communities. One of the more disturbing aspects of these popular crime fictions is the recurrence of the figure of the Jewish collaborator, a figure who denounces other Jewish characters to the authorities and expresses no remorse and little sense of guilt. How might these figurations of Jewish culpability be read? On one level, such fictional representations could be said to confirm the existence of continuing post-war anti-Semitism in their stereotypical depiction of greed, avarice and betrayal within uniquely Jewish communities. Secondly, they might be said to reflect the memory politics of the late 1950s and early 1960s, transitional years in which war stories of French heroism were in the ascendancy. French characters and France as a nation assume no guilt in these crime fictions. Rather, particularist interpretations of war crimes are evoked in which crimes against Jews are committed by Jews.

However, it is also productive to focus on how such popular fictions might relate to broader notions of national guilt, responsibility and recognition of wartime crimes. For if, as Joan B. Wolf argues, representations of Jews in France provide a discursive screen onto which national debates and traumas are projected, these popular fictions centred on Jewish communities could be said to stand in for the whole. They represent a France split asunder and for which there are no tidy endings and no neat resolutions. These texts enact not so much a forgetting as an implosion of memory as family comes to replace nation as the nexus of memory and as a symbol of national collapse at war's end. In these novels, memories of wartime Jewish persecution are firmly implanted in the fictional private realm but they also impinge upon the wider community and implicate a readership obliged to reflect upon a collective sense of guilt, shame or indifference at such wartime crimes. By the 1980s and 1990s, the memory politics of the Second World War would shift significantly, with a younger generation of French crime writers ready to focus insistently on such forgotten crimes.[43] Shifting the onus of guilt away from the Jewish community itself, novelists, such as Didier Daeninckx, Thierry Jonquet and Konop, investigate a far greater range of French actors and agents of persecution as will be discussed in Chapters 3 and 4 of this study. In so doing, they use the crime genre as a damning indictment of French state culpability in the Holocaust. Yet, as these earlier novels demonstrate, wartime crimes against the Jewish community in France were never forgotten and have been represented with varying degrees of intensity over the post-war period. Why, how and when they have been mobilised offers an insight into the tensions governing discussion of French guilt, perpetration and responsibility. In the context of the 1950s and 1960s, these representations of wartime crimes against Jews help nuance general assumptions that troubling memories of the wartime past had been repressed and make visible the moral dilemmas involved in both remembering and forgetting such a conflicted era.

Notes

1   See Susan Rubin Suleiman, *Crises of Memory and the Second World War* (Cambridge, MA: Harvard University Press, 2006), pp. 217–27.
2   Suleiman, *Crises of Memory*, p. 222.
3   See Henry Rousso, 'Les refoulements (1954–1971)', in *Le Syndrome de Vichy: de 1944 à nos jours* (Paris: Editions du Seuil, 1990), pp. 77–117.
4   See Robert Moeller, *War Stories: The Search for a Useable Past in the Federal Republic of Germany* (Berkeley, CA: University of California Press, 2003), for a study of West German war stories of the 1950s which provides a useful comparative frame of reference.

5   See Michael Rothberg's *Multidirectional Memory: Remembering the Holo-caust in the Age of Decolonization* (Palo Alto, CA: Stanford University Press, 2009) for a pioneering study of the intersections between memories of the Holocaust and decolonisation.

6   See Leah D. Hewitt, 'Transitions before the "sorrow": criticism and myth in the late 1950s and early 1960s', in *Remembering the Occupation in French Film: National Identity in Postwar Europe* (Basingstoke: Palgrave Macmillan, 2008), pp. 35–64, for a discussion of war memories in these years via the prism of film.

7   Hewitt, *Remembering the Occupation in French Film*, p. 36.

8   Pieter Lagrou, *The Legacy of Nazi Occupation: Patriotic Memory and National Recovery in Western Europe, 1945–1965* (Cambridge: Cambridge University Press, 2000), p. 252.

9   Annette Wieviorka, 'Jewish identity in the first accounts by extermination camp survivors from France', *Yale French Studies*, 85 (1994), 135–51.

10   Hewitt, *Remembering the Occupation in French Film*, p. 43.

11   Joan B. Wolf, *Harnessing the Holocaust: The Politics of Memory in France* (Palo Alto, CA: Stanford University Press, 2004), p. 14.

12   Nadine Rozenberg Akoun, 'L'Image du juif dans le roman policier français au XXème siècle: évolution et permanence' (Ph.D. dissertation, Université Paris VIII, 2004).

13   For an overview of these cultural motifs in English detective fiction, see Malcolm J. Turnbull, *Victims or Villains: Jewish Images in Classic English Detective Fiction* (Bowling Green, OH: Bowling Green University Popular Press, 1998).

14   André Héléna, *Les Clients du Central Hôtel* (Paris: Editions E-Dite, 2000), p. 66 (And he was Jewish. That hadn't stopped him going to school with the kids in his district, learning to make a basic living, paying his taxes like everyone else and going to war with the others).

15   Nadia Dhoukar, 'Préface', *Léo Malet: Nestor Burma, Les Nouveaux Mystères de Paris II* (Paris: Editions Robert Laffont, 2006), pp. xxxix–xl (The Second World War and the Algerian War leave their traces in the consciences of men, as well as on their environment).

16   *Du rébecca rue des Rosiers* (Paris: Robert Laffont, 1958). Subsequent editions: Paris: Livre de poche, 1977; Paris: Fleuve noir, 1984, 1987 and 1995; Paris: Presses de la Cité, 1990; Paris: U.G.E, 1987; Paris: Robert Laffont, 2006. *Des kilomètres de linceuls* (Paris: Robert Laffont, 1955). Subsequent editions: Paris: Livre de poche, 1976; Paris: Fleuve noir, 1982 and 1994; Paris: Presses de la Cité, 1989; Paris: U.G.E., 1988; Paris: Robert Laffont, 2006.

17   Karen Adler describes the rue des Rosiers as 'the Jewish quarter not merely of Paris but it might be suggested of France itself', *Jews and Gender in Liberation France* (Cambridge: Cambridge University Press, 2003), p. 146. The Sentier district is reputed for its clothing and footware manufacture, one

area of commercial activity closely associated with Jewish migrant communities.

18 The question of Burma's, and by implication, Malet's, xenophobia and racism is addressed by Dhoukar in her preface to *Léo Malet*, pp. xli–xlvi, and by Michelle Emanuel, *From Surrealism to Less-Exquisite Cadavers: Léo Malet and the Evolution of the French Roman Noir* (Amsterdam: Rodopi, 2006), pp. 90–5.

19 See *Du rébecca rue des Rosiers* in Léo Malet, *Léo Malet: Nestor Burma, Les Nouveaux Mystères de Paris I* (Paris: Editions Robert Laffont, 2006). All further references will be to this edition. Rachel Blum is referred to by Baget as 'la youpine' (the yid) (p. 122). Faroux, the sympathetic police inspector, referring to Jewish names comments 'ils appellent tous comme ça dans la tribu' (they are all called that in the tribe) (p. 177) and a secondary Jewish character in a brothel is described as following: 'il lève sur nous des yeux de velours et un tarin comme on n'en voit que sur les caricatures anti-sémites' (he turned his doe eyes upon us with a nose that you only see in anti-Semitic caricatures) (p. 163).

20 The reference is made explicit on p. 182. Joseph Joanovici was a well-known Jewish collaborator who supplied Germans with scrap metal as part of a network of contacts between the German authorities and the Parisian underworld. See Bertram M. Gordon (ed.), *Historical Dictionary of World War II France: The Occupation, Vichy and the Resistance, 1938–1946* (Westport, CT: Greenwood Press, 1998), p. 267.

21 In André Halimi's *La Délation sous l'occupation* (Paris: L'Harmattan, 1983), Halimi provides an account of the many letters of denunciation sent by French people to various French and German authorities during the occupation. He surmises that at least three million letters were received by the German Kommandatur alone, the primary aim being denunciation of Jews. There is no discussion in his study of Jewish auto-denunciation, which makes the use of this trope in French crime fiction even more perplexing for an informed reader.

22 Malet, *Du rébecca rue des Rosiers*, p. 225 (The house in question was truly sinister, as poisonous as they come, particularly at this twilight hour and in the drizzling rain. Paint was peeling off the façade. It was three storeys high and all the windows were walled up. One of the monumental wooden door panels was covered in posters, mostly in Hebrew, and in chalked writings. On the other was nailed an enamelled sign: DANGER).

23 See Joan B. Wolf, 'Anne Frank is dead, long live Anne Frank: the 6-day war and the origins of Holocaust consciousness', in *Harnessing the Holocaust*, pp. 25–50, for a discussion of the early memory politics of French responses to the Holocaust. As Wolf argues, such narratives of Jewish redemption would be superseded by traumatic accounts of wartime loss in the aftermath of the Six-Day War in 1967.

24   Malet, *Des kilomètres de linceuls*, p. 256 (Esther, she corrected dryly. Alice is a Gentile name. Esther, that's a real Jewish name. I am a hideous and vile Jew. If I hadn't been Jewish, none of what happened to me would have happened.)

25   Malet, *Des kilomètres de linceuls*, p. 287 (I had to get by on my own, and act quickly, with a chance of success so slight that it might too be returning from the deportation camps).

26   Malet, *Des kilomètres de linceuls*, p. 353 (Berglevy Fabrics. Cotton fabrics, Silks, Woollens. Linens. Cinema screens for dreams? Bed sheets for love? Shrouds, nothing but shrouds.)

27   Rozenberg Akoun, 'L'Image du juif dans le roman policier français au XXème siècle', p. 112 (contradicts the hypothesis … according to which the immediate post-war period, the *trente glorieuses*, was a time of denial and forgetting of the occupation).

28   The novel was also later adapted for French television as *Le Retour d'Elisabeth Wolf* (1982), directed by Josée Dayan.

29   Hubert Monteilhet, *Le Retour des cendres* (Paris: Denoël, 1961). Subsequent editions are: Paris: Denoël, 1966; Paris: Livre de poche, 1967; Paris Editions J'ai Lu, 1977; Paris: Librairie générale française, 1992; Paris: Editions de Fallois, 2008.

30   The quotation is: 'a faint cold fear thrills through my veins', from *Romeo and Juliet*, Act 4, Scene 3. Hubert Monteilhet has had a successful career as an author of psychological thrillers and historical crime fiction. He was awarded the Grand Prix de littérature policière for his first crime novel, *Les Mantes religieuses* (1960), and has returned to the occupation period in novels such as *La Perte de vue: roman du temps de la Kollaboration* (1986), *Non-sens* (1971) and *Choc en retour* (2009). These novels all focus to a greater or lesser extent on crimes of collaboration and their consequences.

31   See Bryan Cheyette, 'Introduction: semitism and the cultural realm', in *Constructions of 'the Jew' in English Literature and Society: Racial Representations 1875–1945* (Cambridge: Cambridge University Press, 1993), pp. 1–12, for a discussion of Jewish representations and cultural identity.

32   Hubert Monteilhet, *Omnibus* (Paris: Editions de Fallois, 2008), *Le Retour des cendres*, p. 141. All further references will be to this edition. All English translations will be taken from Hubert Monteilhet, *Return from the Ashes*, trans. Tony White (London: Panther Books Ltd, 1965), 'a community of suffering that has been cemented by the years', p. 29

33   Monteilhet, *Le Retour des cendres*, p. 134. 'I had almost forgotten who I was. I was severely reminded of it. I mean to stay aware of the reminder', *Return from the Ashes*, p. 19.

34   A similar process of disclosure and disavowal of Jewish identity is highlighted in Francis Didelot's *Dernier Matin* (1959) as wartime and post-war

denunciation and murder are revealed to be the result of the shame of dis-
covering Jewish ancestry.

35 Monteilhet, *Le Retour des cendres*, p. 141. 'You think that you are a Jew and
lots of dangerous idiots have the same illusion about you. Being an Israeli-
te's like being a Christian, being a Jew is like being a Frenchman. It's all in
the mind', *Return from the Ashes*, pp. 28–9.

36 Monteilhet, *Le Retour des cendres*, p. 142. 'I believe that you suffer for nothing, he [Stan] agreed sadly. I know that it's very hard to suffer that way but
it's better than giving your troubles a spurious meaning. It's nobler', *Return
from the Ashes*, p. 29.

37 Monteilhet, *Le Retour des cendres*, p. 219. 'I also felt that it was nobler to
hand my wife over to soldiers. The more gentlemen there are involved in a
crime, the less bitter the taste it leaves', *Return from the Ashes*, p. 126.

38 Monteilhet, *Le Retour des cendres*, p. 219. 'It was not easy, at the time, to
imagine what a concentration camp under a dictator was really like', *Return
from the Ashes*, p. 127.

39 This term is used by Robert Moeller in his study of West German war narratives, *War Stories*, p. 17.

40 Tzvetan Todorov, *Facing the Extreme: Moral Life in the Concentration Camps*
(New York: Henry Holt, 1996).

41 Adler, *Jews and Gender in Liberation France*, p. 154.

42 Monteilhet, *Le Retour des cendres*, p. 127. A child is thrown from a moving
train by its sibling. Elisabeth Wolf merely moves carriage.

43 For a discussion of representations of Jewish characters and the occupation in post–1980 French fiction, see Margaret-Anne Hutton, 'From christ-
killers to christ-figures: representations of Jews in post-1980 French occupation fiction', *French Cultural Studies*, 18:1 (2007), 107–24.

3

Resurgent collaboration: revisiting collaboration in French crime fiction of the 1980s

French collaboration with the occupier was one of a number of war stories that resurfaced sporadically in the immediate post-war decades in the form of high-profile political and legal affairs.[1] Such public airings served to remind people of the reverberations of wartime choices, although collaboration was ever the shadowy other of dominant resistance narratives of national heroism. Even into the 1970s and early 1980s, leading historians were still able to contend that collaboration was 'taboo', a 'sensitive subject' and generated 'embarrassed silence' and 'persistent reticence' from many French people.[2] However, as this chapter will demonstrate, fictional representations of collaboration were never absent from the cultural sphere and remained wedded to a set of narrative tropes and associations that would repeat over the post-war period. What changed perceptions of collaboration in the 1970s and 1980s was the work of a new generation of historians, writers and filmmakers who were prepared to question and contest previously accepted views. In the field of crime fiction, this resurgence of interest accentuated the multi-faceted nature of collaboration and the troubling legacy it would bequeath succeeding generations.

This chapter will begin by examining the early representations of collaboration in Sartre's influential essay 'Qu'est-ce qu'un collaborateur?' It will discuss motifs and cultural stereotypes of collaboration in pro-resistance fictions of the late 1940s and their counterpoint in the work of writers who offer a morally conflicted picture of wartime France and collaboration. The chapter will then proceed to analyse the revisionist readings of collaboration proposed by historians of the 1970s and the 1980s and the literary and cultural responses to such shifts in historical understanding, specifically in the work of writers of the *mode rétro*. It is their fraught confrontations with a missing wartime inheritance of collaboration that frames this chapter's reading of three French crime novels of the 1980s. Finally, this chapter will explore novels by Jean Mazarin, Georges-Jean Arnaud and Didier Daeninckx, all of whom engage with the questions raised by historians, writers and filmmakers on the scope, reach and diversity of collaboration. Who were the collaborators? What did they do? Which legacy do they bequeath successor generations? In all instances, crime fiction dramatises questions of guilt, responsibility and justice and the intergenerational burden of the secret of collaboration. As interventions in memory debates, such novels demonstrate the extent to which popular culture has popularised historical reassessments of the past and how, in the narrative template of crime fiction, such reassessments gain a heightened emotional and ethical charge.

Histories, memories and fictions of collaboration

The most famous examination of collaboration in the immediate aftermath of war was Sartre's 1945 'Qu'est-ce qu'un collaborator?' As Susan Suleiman contends in her analysis of Sartre as a memoirist of occupied France, such an article was intended to bolster images of French unanimity under occupation, even if this meant leaving aside contentious aspects of France's wartime record.[3] In this context, 'Qu'est-ce qu'un collaborateur?' can be read as contributing to a general minimisation of French collaboration in the early post-war years. In Sartre's article, the collaborator is analysed predominantly in social and psychological terms as an 'unintegrated' individual whose wartime choices cannot be attributed to class or group affiliations.[4] Instead, Sartre builds a picture of collaboration as individual pathology, an illness or condition that is exacerbated by the conditions of war and national crisis. An extremely small grouping (Sartre estimates their numbers to be in the region of 2 per cent), collaborators are positioned on the social and political margins of the national community. The features shared by these individuals are: a rejection of French Republicanism and democracy; a fascination with the violence of dictatorial rule; an attraction to foreign models of authority; and submission to the exigencies of historical events (the victory of Germany) over proactive engagement with the forces for change. In addition, Sartre casts the collaborator in overtly sexualised terms as 'un curieux mélange de masochisme et d'homosexualité', men attracted to the virile ideal of the German warrior and who perform as the feminine partner in a metaphorical union of nations.[5] In this optic, collaboration is expunged from the nation as the fact of a small group of weak and submissive men whose actions in no way reflect upon the fortitude and suffering of a resilient France.

Such a formulation of collaboration, as individual pathology, personal failings and sexual submission, circulated widely in pro-resistance fiction published in the immediate post-war years. For Michael Kelly: 'most fictional narratives which dealt with the question of collaboration tended to use the sexual connection'.[6] This was evident in collaboration's presentation as 'irresistible coercion' or 'yielding to a seduction'.[7] Whether authors chose to focus on the individual psychology of the collaborator or the base opportunism of collusion with the enemy, a second common denominator of such early fictions, for Kelly, was their limited discussion of who collaborators were and what they had done. Collaboration was cast as personal choice and poor individual judgement to the detriment of explanations that explored the political and ideological contexts which made collaboration a reasoned response to occupation for considerable sections of French society. Yet, as Kelly and others have noted, dissonant voices and representations were also evident in the late 1940s from writers who, if not exonerating collaboration, were prepared to argue that it was perhaps no worse than other wartime choices. This is the case of Marcel Aymé whose novel *Uranus* (1948) provides a vehement critique of the arbitrariness of post-war justice.[8] While one cannot discount the political agenda subtending such representations, Aymé's novel emphasises the varied forms collaboration took – economic, ideological and social/quotidian – and the passivity and self-interest of the French population under occupation, presenting a vision of France in which there are no heroes and certainly no innocents.[9] Sartrean constructions of collaboration may well have conformed to the epic narratives of resistance promoted by those in power but such writings did not mean that other fictional representations were not attuned to the fact that acts of collaboration had been a feature of wartime life.

By the late 1960s and early 1970s, cultural stereotypes of collaboration as either individual aberration or mass passivity and self-interest in the face of German occupation were being questioned and contested. Historians, such as Robert Paxton, paved the way for a radical reassessment of collaboration at a national level, figured in the Vichy regime and its leading political figures. For Paxton promoted the view that Vichy could no longer be regarded as 'culpable defeatism' or 'prudent caution', shielding France from the worst excesses of German occupation.[10] Rather, he integrated Vichy into a broader historical continuum of conflict between opposing ideological factions in France that stretched back to the French

Revolution. He questioned the notion that Vichy was the lesser evil facing defeated France, setting up a moral balance sheet that condemned the regime for its sectarian use of defeat; for the ways in which it had abetted internal dissent; and for its complicity and collusion with the German occupier, in relation to the forced labour scheme and the deportation of Jews. As Paxton's prose style made evident, he was putting the case for the prosecution and one which was based not only on historical facts but also on a sense of unresolved conflicts and the need for France to assume moral responsibility for its past: summarising his views in the preface to the 1981 re-edition of his study, Paxton stated: 'Emotionally, the Vichy regime has not yet been reintegrated into any consistent sense of past'.[11]

Other historians of the 1970s and 1980s also approached collaboration via politically and ideologically inflected readings. Collaboration was perceived neither to be predestined nor solely the result of self-interest and opportunism but the outcome of many disparate personal and political factors. In his study of collaborators, Pascal Ory highlighted the influence of preceding collective traumas, such as the First World War and the Russian Revolution of 1914; the desire for order at a time of crisis; and the profound misunderstanding, on the part of many committed French collaborators, of the ends of German National Socialism. For the Nazi invader, the aim was not partnership with the occupied countries of Western Europe but rather submission and exploitation. Bertram M. Gordon plotted similar patterns of collaboration, including collaborators' romantic identification with German virility and the experience of combat; a belief in the need for order and a misguided faith in the promises of the German occupier. In addition, Gerhard Hirschfeld emphasised the rivalries and inconsistencies within the German institutions and organisations active in occupied France: 'a history of the collaboration of the people of an occupied country is always a history of the occupying power as well'.[12] What emerges in these historically revisionist accounts of the 1970s and early 1980s is a perception of collaboration as a multifarious set of wartime attitudes and actions that cannot be divorced from political, economic, social and cultural contexts, both within and beyond France. It is these contexts that give collaboration meaning as both an individual choice and a collective phenomenon.

At the same time as collaboration was undergoing reinvestigation by a new generation of historians, parallel shifts were taking place in literary and cultural domains. The limited release of the documentary film *Le Chagrin et la pitié* (1969) in France in 1971 is often cited as the turning point in public perceptions of the war years. Director Marcel Ophuls' depiction of life under occupation in Clermont-Ferrand was a revelation for its deliberate attempt to demystify what Ophuls and his producers, André Harris and Alain de Sédouy, saw as exaggerated accounts of resistance heroism. Interviewing former German army officers, ideological collaborators, Jewish survivors, local resisters and prominent political personalities, the documentary left viewers with a composite and ambiguous image of life under occupation. This was not a France of resisters, focused on the well-known figures from the Free French who had dominated the airwaves until this point, but rather a wartime France of internal divisions, indigenous anti-Semitism and where heroes, victims and persecutors could not always be easily distinguished.[13]

Le Chagrin et la pitié inaugurated, albeit unintentionally, what has become known as the *mode rétro*, a wave of novels, memoirs and films from the late 1960s to the early 1980s that were perceived to challenge the dominance of the heroic resistance narratives of the early post-war decades. As Alan Morris notes in his wide-ranging study of the prose fiction of the *mode rétro*, this contestatory position was not new; challenges to the pre-eminence of the resistance epic had been in circulation since the end of hostilities and were visible in a range of prose fictions from the late 1940s onwards.[14] What was new was the public receptivity to such counter-narratives. Morris attributes this to two key factors: the departure of de Gaulle from politics and public life, a figure identified as the post-war architect of the resistance epic, and the coming of age of a new generation of writers, filmmakers and cultural critics who allowed different voices and wartime experiences to be heard. These figures represented, for Morris, a 'generation of orphans' embarked on a quest to discover more about a missing national and familial past.[15]

In many ways, it is this 'generation of orphans' which offers the most telling insights into the reinvestigation of collaboration in France in the 1970s and 1980s. Authors, such as Patrick Modiano, produced meticulously researched narratives of the war years that drew on history, biography and fiction to create a kaleidoscopic vision of the wartime past.[16] What was missing in such fictions was often a parental figure whose problematic wartime past had been erased from family or national memory. In a number of cases, this was the past of a collaborating father. Marie Chaix, Evelyne Le Garrec, Pascal Jardin and Jean-Luc Maxence all published novels in these years that grappled with the incomplete transmission of such a parental heritage.[17] Whether the response took the form of an attempt at rehabilitation, even an apologia for past actions, or a vigorous denunciation and distancing from the actions of such a parent, all these authors immersed themselves in the war years in order to investigate the past of a shadowy parental figure. Like their historian counterparts of the same period, such authors sought to take stock of the past; to consider questions of collective guilt and responsibility; to acknowledge the failure of accepted authority figures, both familial and national; and to address the treatment of Jews in occupied France. Such investigations were necessarily as much an imaginative endeavour as a factual one, the break in the relay of intergenerational memory having created a void which could be bridged only by the processes of writing. Such writing projects allowed these authors simultaneously to reconnect with a family past of collaboration and to purge themselves of its oppressive legacy. Pivotal to all of these fictional texts was the choice of a narrative form that could accommodate the fraught intersection of historical and autobiographical material or, as Colin Nettelbeck notes, 'a story that might carry the history'.[18] One such story to dramatise these dilemmas was crime fiction.

French crime fiction of the 1970s and 1980s proved itself to be acutely aware of the reassessments of collaboration taking place in these decades.[19] A number of authors, such as Jean Mazarin, Georges-Jean Arnaud and Didier Daeninckx, produced novels that presented collaboration as a complex historical phenomenon that took many forms and permeated all strata of French society. Their novels also address collaboration's legacy for those who come after, the 'generation of orphans', and its impact on contemporary social and political relations. This chapter will analyse the contribution of three novels to debates over the nature and legacy of collaboration in 1980s France: Jean Mazarin's *Collabo-Song* (1981), Georges-Jean Arnaud's *Maudit Blood* (1985) and Didier Daeninckx's *Meurtres pour mémoire* (1984).[20] It will examine these novels along three axes: firstly, it will examine how these novels construct collaboration. Who are the collaborators? What are their crimes? What are their motivations and how can such motivations be understood in political, personal or ideological terms? Secondly, the chapter will relate such questioning to the legacies of collaboration. How is such a shameful personal and political history transmitted to succeeding generations? What are the perils of transmission (or non-transmission)? How do second-generation protagonists construct a sense of identity in the shadow of such a heritage? Integral to these considerations will be the framing of collaboration in terms of crime, guilt and responsibility for the persecution of Jews in France. As if in response to the question posed by Sartre in 1945, 'Qu'est-ce qu'un collaborator?', the answer in these novels moves from the singular to the plural. Collaborators are many, varied and unexpected and their destiny is, in all cases, bound up with their wartime other, the Jew.

Remémorations, interrogations, fascinations[21]

Jean Mazarin's *Collabo-Song* (1981) follows the occupation itinerary of a young Parisian housewife, Laure Santenac, and the circulation of post-war myths and memories surrounding her sudden disappearance in the spring of 1943.[22] The novel is divided into four sections: 'A propos de Laure Santenac', sets in place a present-day investigation into the war-time history and mysterious death of the main protagonist. The subsequent three sections immerse the reader in the war years themselves, reconstructed via Laure's point of view and headed: 'Le premier cercle (Printemps 1942)', 'La spirale (Eté 1942–Printemps 1943)' and 'Le dernier cercle (Printemps 1943)'. Her fictive biography is, therefore, one that traces her individual spiral downwards and frames her choice of collaboration in circular metaphors that suggest both a Dantesque image of the concentric circles of hell and also the circularity of the text as it begins and ends with presumptions on Laure's attitudes and implication in collaboration.[23] In this sense, *Collabo-Song* offers a kaleidoscopic, and often morally troubling, evocation of collaboration and the intense difficulty of resolving, many years later, issues of guilt and responsibility.

Laure begins the wartime narrative as a bored housewife, trapped in a sterile and loveless marriage, having suffered a miscarriage that ends all hope of children. This image of the childless woman becomes one, over the course of the novel, which gathers symbolic importance as a representation of a damaged nation, doomed to obsolescence and unable to transmit a meaningful wartime legacy to succeeding generations. Yet it is via the personal relationships of the main protagonist that the narrative charts the broad phases of collective support for collaboration and the shifts in power base and personality at Vichy.[24] Firstly, Laure's relationship with Edouard, her older husband, gestures at the breakdown of established social and political hierarchies in the face of defeat and the early accommodation of occupation. This 'époque entre parenthèses', as one character terms it,[25] sees Edouard's adultery sanctioned as long as social appearances are retained. His successful career as a surgeon continues under German directives and control. The occupation and the early politics of collaboration are represented here as a marriage of convenience from which both parties profit financially if not emotionally. Laure's first lover, journalist Pierre Boulard, mirrors a movement from passive acceptance of occupation to more active participation in the politics of collaboration via affirmation of Vichy ideals. A writer for the collaborationist press, Pierre embodies an early phase of support for the National Revolution and its traditionalist values of family, work and fatherland. Pierre's increasing disillusionment with the corruption and political infighting at Vichy is translated into admiration for the activities of the Waffen-SS and the war on the Eastern Front, suggestive of a fascination with the virile brotherhood of arms and the sway of foreign power that resonates with Sartre's early article on the collaborator. It is with Laure's third and final lover, Bernard de Monsoult, a French Gestapist, that the novel veers towards the horrors of the final years of Vichy as a police state, with the rise of the French militia and the torture of resisters and Jews. Overt displays of allegiance to the German invader in the last days of occupation provide a damning fictional indictment of a regime and its acolytes given over to the worse excesses of greed, violence and inhumanity.

One of the innovations of *Collabo-Song* is to plot this intersection of the personal and the political under occupation via the viewpoint of a female protagonist. The narrative reconfigures the dominant sexualised metaphors of French submission to the occupier that marked much 1940s cultural production. Here, the collaborator is female but the emphasis is not on seduction and coercion but rather agency, choice and responsibility. This is most evident in the counterpoint to the story of collaboration in the novel: that of anti-Semitism. The narrative of *Collabo-Song* sets out swiftly the banality of anti-Semitism in occupied France as Edouard is able to continue his career as a surgeon due to the support of Professeur Lebastien: 'Il [Edouard] le savait anti-sémite, mais pas plus que bien d'autres de ses confrères'.[26] The impact of this ambient anti-Semitism is confirmed by Laure's first active engagement with collaboration: her anonymous denunciation of her maid Mireille/Rosette whom she supposes to be Jewish, having discovered tracts in her room warning Jews of impending police round-ups.[27] Having until this point displayed Laure as impervious to the politics and ideological context of war, the narrative changes to present her as choosing to denounce both maid and husband (she places tracts in his bureau) for the most selfish of reasons: a desire to be rid of her husband and anxiety over her own safety as she fears guilt by association with pro-resistance activism. This act of denunciation is the tipping point for Laure, intertwining the personal and the political in ways that refute an easy disassociation of national shame and personal responsibility. Her act has fatal consequences for Edouard who is arrested and is later reported to have committed suicide by throwing himself from the window of French Gestapo headquarters.

Yet the narrative twists and turns of the novel collude to undermine a polarised reading of persecutor and victim. Laure's opposite in the text, the betrayed Mireille/Rosette, is recast by Mazarin to offer a fractured sense of both national politics and personal choices. For it transpires that Mireille is in fact a German informer, placed in the Santenac household in order to spy upon Edouard whom we learn may be the leader of a nascent Gaullist resistance network. The original Mireille is Rosette Goldenberg, a Jewish student and resister, who has been charged with fermenting opposition to the impending round-up of Jews in Paris and who is arrested, and the reader assumes murdered, preceding the events of the novel. It is her German substitute who takes her place in the resistance network and her post in the Santenac household. Post-war, with only fragments of information, Rosette Goldenberg and her German substitute are elided. Rosette is assumed to have denounced her fellow Jewish resisters when the network is decimated and is condemned as a double agent, a clichéd stereotype of the collaborating Jew. Yet, in an ironic twist of fate, Laure, the collaborator, ends her life as a Jew, having taken up the suggestion of her lover Bernard Monsoult to pose as Jewish and to use a Jewish escape network, organised by the unassuming Dr Eugène, should the tide of war turn against them. Laure's false identity (she presents herself as Laura Goldenberg) reconnects the two women and seals her fate as the reader learns in an epilogue that Laure disappears in 1943, one of the sixty-three people whom the infamous Dr Marcel Petiot assassinated in his apartment with the promise of escape from occupied France.

The intersections of collaboration and anti-Semitism and persecution and victimisation as personified in the two main female protagonists of the novel clearly mark Mazarin's preoccupation with the impossibilities of determining occupation choices and identities with any certainty many years later. Laure, the wife of a Gaullist hero, a denouncer of Jews, the mistress of a Gestapo torturer and the Jewish victim of Dr Petiot, signals the multiplicity of French wartime legacies and the dangers of seeking moral absolutes in a time of crisis. Indeed, the issue of transmission is evident in the novel in its opening section when a series of present-day witnesses give testimony to an anonymous extra-diegetic narrator on the lives and reputations of Laure Santenac and Rosette Goldenberg. On the one hand, there is denial of collaboration and its crimes. Laure's second lover, Paul-Alexandre Berlanger, denies any meaningful relationship with her, a statement disproved by the later text, and her crimes are rejected as mere fabulation. On the other, there is misrepresentation and ignorance of the victims of collaboration, such as Rosette, whose name is taboo, even for close relatives, as a suspected collaborator. What has occurred, the narrative suggests, is a blurring of boundaries and a confusion of trajectories which lead to falsehoods and myth-making. As the first witness claims: 'tout n'a peut-être été pas si blanc ou si noir!'[28]

Collaboration is presented in *Collabo-Song* as a complex and multifaceted phenomenon. Via the use of a female protagonist and her implication within the structures and organisations of collaborationist France, Mazarin illustrates how difficult it is to separate the personal from the political. Laure Santenac personifies a national community drawn increasingly to the power and prestige of collaboration but ever alert to its own needs and interests. Yet, the interplay of Laure Santenac and her Jewish alter-ego Laura Goldenberg poignantly captures how such choices carried with them catastrophic outcomes for communities excluded from the Vichy regime's vision of France; a choice of active collaboration was inevitably a choice to support, tacitly or not, the persecution of Jews in France. In terms of evaluating the crimes of the wartime past, *Collabo-Song* highlights the transmission difficulties encountered by post-war generations. As the voices of present-day witnesses suggest at the beginning of the text, black and white judgements on the past are hard to sustain, above all as those who can corroborate such truths may well be at pains to hide them.

In Georges-Jean Arnaud's *Maudit Blood*, the narrative focus shifts from representations of collaboration during the war years to the perils of non-transmission of the past for succeeding generations.[29] The novel is centred on a respectable bourgeois couple, Louise and Etienne Marchand, and their adopted daughter Charlotte, a student in Nice. Yet, the apparently anodyne life of Louise and Etienne is revealed to be a façade as the reader learns that, over forty years earlier, they, with other relatives of the Savetan family, on the family farm near Toulouse, murdered Jews lured there with the promise of escape to Spain. Following the Liberation, Louise and Etienne abandoned the family farm with their share of the family's wartime gains, seeking to erase their wartime past and to protect their daughter by claiming that she is adopted. However, the past surges back into the present in the form of Emma and Eloi, Louise's brother and sister, who track down the Marchands and ransom Charlotte in order to steal the Marchands' remaining war booty and to pull them back into the orbit of the violent and dysfunctional Savetan clan.

In contrast to *Collabo-Song*, collaboration in *Maudit Blood* is represented as a conscious ideological choice that connects with present-day right-wing extremism. The spectre of Pétain looms large as a rallying point for a network of former collaborators and French Gestapists who feel excluded from the national community and are united in their sense of injustice at being on the losing side of a *guerre franco-française* that continues unabated if clandestinely. Indeed, the Savetans's wartime crimes are not presented as mere wartime opportunism. They resonate with a deep history of French anti-Semitism that has been translated into new forms of persecution and exclusion of others, here imaged as North-African immigrants. References to the campaigns of Simon Wiesenthal and Beate Klarsfeld to locate war criminals; the unease and anger at the forthcoming trial of Klaus Barbie and revelations of the occupation activities of Maurice Papon, all suggest a construction of wartime collaboration as part of a broad ideological conflict centred on questions of race, nation and identity.[30]

In *Maudit Blood*, what generates and sustains such a construction of politically and ideologically inspired collaboration is a story of family dysfunctionality. As in *Collabo-Song*, this is allied with the trajectory of the wartime other, the Jew. The figures of Louise and Etienne are haunted by their past, forced to abandon home and fake identities at the merest hint that family members may have discovered their new lives. They are throughout the narrative presented as persecuted peoples whose post-war lives mirror the flight and fear of the Jewish victims they wish to forget. This is taken to its logical conclusion as Arnaud constructs an image of the Savetan family replicating the persecutory regime of the concentration camp in their own home. In their desire to punish Louise and Etienne for abandoning the family and the wartime past, the Savetans plan to imprison them in the family home on rue Alsace-Lorraine as domestic slaves in a perverted image of the *univers concentrationnaire*: 'Pire comme un camp de concentration. Auschwitz à domicile dans une aussi jolie ville que Toulouse, l'horreur rue Alsace-Lorraine avec des kapos aussi féroces que ceux d'autrefois.'[31] Yet, none of this detracts from the narrative ambiguity of the presentation of Louise and Etienne. Although the reader can sympathise with their intention to start afresh, the consequences of their repression of the past are evident in the depiction of Emma and Eloi, their familial persecutors, and the trajectory of their daughter, Charlotte.

The representation of Emma and Eloi offers the reader a phantasmagorical evocation of the return of the repressed. Presented as greedy, acquisitive and ill-educated, they are the monstrous double of Louise and Etienne. Arnaud presents them as trapped in the past; Emma still wearing the stolen fur coat of one of her wartime Jewish victims and Eloi wielding the penknife with which he slit their throats. In the Nice section of the novel, they are the source of hilarity in restaurants for the serving staff as they eat immoderately and with few table manners. Their inability to operate new technology, such as the answering machine, identifies their anachronistic nature. They inspire a form of physical repulsion in others, particularly Emma whose unctuous voice and fetid breath lead both Louise and Charlotte to vomit in her presence. As symbols of collaboration, they make visible the past that Louise and Etienne have attempted so carefully to conceal: an anti-modern, regressive and malevolent heritage that erupts sporadically in the present.

However, the novel is at its most condemnatory of Louise and Etienne when it addresses the consequences of the non-transmission of the past for the next generation. Louise and Etienne have fabricated a story of childlessness in order to distance Charlotte from her past and to mask their own wartime actions; a much-loved daughter has been led to think of herself as a substitute and consolation for children lost in early infancy. As her parents's story of adoption starts to unravel, Charlotte begins to confess her confusion and emotional distress at her uncertain origins. A sense of dispossession and a lack of understanding lead to Charlotte assuming the position of the 'orphaned generation'. Unsure about her past and with a damaged sense of self, Charlotte is vulnerable to the wartime narratives of others, such as Emma and Eloi, and easy prey for their plans to trap her parents. As the narrative makes clear, it is impossible to cast off the crimes of the past as Louise and Etienne had intended. Such memories resurface in the monstrous guise of Emma and Eloi and haunt the narrative in images of illness and disease. For, as the narrator comments, on hearing Emma's voice, it is for Charlotte 'comme si au bout de vingt ans un souvenir antérieur à sa naissance s'était fixé en elle comme une tumeur maligne ...'.[32] This image of collaboration as a hidden growth or tumour on the body politic is developed further in the text in Arnaud's image of collaboration as a blood crime which infects the present.

In *Maudit Blood*, the narrative of collaboration and its place in French society and history is connected to the family history of the Savetans as haemophiliacs. Léontine, the family matriarch, has forbidden procreation in order to prevent detection of the family by those seeking war criminals via an international database of haemophiliacs. Yet the connotations of the metaphor of a blood crime go far beyond this. Haemophilia, as a disease passed down through male descendants, points to the sterility of collaboration, a wartime phenomenon which can have no productive outcome. In the narrative economy of the novel, haemophilia is represented as a cursed genetic inheritance that damns the family to extinction and represents, to Léontine, at least a form of divine retribution and just desserts for the murder of hundreds of Jews: 'On avait tué du Juif au nom de la cupidité mais surtout, au départ, par conviction chrétienne anachronique. Il fallait des bourreaux pour cette tâche mais les exécuteurs devaient également périr.'[33] In a deliberate inversion of anti-Semitic propaganda, it is the Savetans who are the damned race condemned to a form of 'autogénocide',[34] as, in the last pages of the novel, Louise and Etienne end the abusive cycle of blackmail and blow up both the Savetan home in Toulouse and themselves in an act of purification. With the wartime collaborators eliminated, the novel posits the end game of all racist discourse and actions as destruction for victim and persecutor.

However, despite what would appear to be a narrative of non-transmission, the novel ends with continuity: Charlotte has a baby girl, named Louise in memory of her grandmother. The cursed family legacy has been obviated; new life has been created. Yet, the novel's ending is ambiguous: Charlotte is the carrier of the haemophiliac gene and may produce boys. How will her husband pass on the information about family inheritance, information he has concealed from her in another instance of non-transmission? What will be the outcome for baby Louise and the next generation who will carry the burden of the past as both a genetic anomaly and historical shame?

In *Maudit Blood*, collaboration is cast as politically and ideologically motivated and capable of generating a legacy which has implications for political activism in the present. Like *Collabo-Song*, this is filtered through personal relations and a family narrative which makes clear that non-transmission of the past can be corrosive not only for those who carry responsibility for such acts but for those born after, such as Charlotte and her daughter Louise. The use of the metaphor of haemophilia and the notion of a blood crime transmissible through the family line highlights yet further that collaboration cannot be erased from the national or familial record. By coupling politics and genetics, the novel suggests that collaboration remains deeply embedded in French social and political life and will continue to impact upon future generations until its meaning and consequences are confronted.

In the final novel in this chapter, Didier Daeninckx's *Meurtres pour mémoire* (1984), the reader encounters a further formulation of collaboration which probes the repercussions of the wartime past on post-war histories of France, above all decolonisation. Republished nine times to date, Daeninckx's second published novel, *Meurtres pour mémoire*, has had phenomenal success as a crime novel.[35] Within the first two years of publication, it had sold over 40,000 copies. The novel was awarded the Grand prix de littérature policière in 1985, the Prix Paul Vaillant-Couturier in 1984; was broadcast as a television film in 1985, directed by Laurent Heynemann, and was adapted as a graphic novel in 1991. It has built Daeninckx's reputation as the 'Michelet of the Série noire'.[36]

Meurtres pour mémoire follows the investigation of Inspector Cadin who is charged with solving the murder of a young history student, Bernard Thiraud, in Toulouse in the textual present of July 1982. However, in order to identify the culprit of what appears to be a motiveless crime, Cadin is obliged to return to two troubled pasts: the first, French state complicity in the deportation of Jews during the Second World War, and the second, the brutal police repression of a peaceful demonstration of North Africans on the streets of Paris on 17 October 1961 opposing draconian curfew measures at the height of the Algerian War. It is during the 1961 demonstration that Bernard's father, Roger Thiraud, is assassinated in a sequence of events which leads to his son's death more than twenty years later. What brings all three time frames into alignment is the figure of the state functionary, André Veillut, a thinly veiled reference to the figure of Maurice Papon, who is responsible for the murder of Bernard and his father, Roger, in a bid to mask his past as a zealous Vichy civil servant who sanctioned the deportation of hundreds of Jewish families from the Midi-Pyrénées region via Drancy to Auschwitz.

In terms of the representation of collaboration, Daeninckx enacts the bold move of locating culpability in the figure of the ultimate arbiter of the state, the civil servant. At the investigation's end, with Veillut assassinated and never to stand trial, Cadin defines Veillut's role in the deportation of Jews not as one born of political conviction or support for anti-Semitism but 'tout simplement en obéissant aux réglements et en exécutant les ordres de la hiérarchie'.[37] Human beings, above all the Jewish children who haunt the text and Cadin's dreams, are viewed as surplus items of stock to be transported abroad in the most efficient manner possible. Indeed, while Veillut offers up the figure of an individual perpetrator to round off Cadin's investigation, the more troubling manifestation of wartime collaboration in the novel is the state system, variously configured as the justice system, the police force or the political system.

For, in each instance, it is when such systems depersonalise a process or treat citizens as little more than statistics on a page that, the novel suggests, abuse, misuse and, ultimately, state-sanctioned mass persecution can develop.

This most potent image of this abuse is offered in the scenes set in the Toulouse municipal archives. Cadin, and his deputy, Lardenne, visit the archives to read the same files which Bernard Thiraud consulted on the day he was murdered. As Cadin and Lardenne flick through the war-time papers filed DE, they appear to offer no illumination with regard to the motives behind the crime: 'DEbroussaillage … DEdommagement … DEfense passive …' while Cadin learns that the 'DElibérations de la DElégation spéciale de Lanta' have been cancelled.[38] Immediately fol-lowing these files comes Deportation, 'traitée de la même manière que les autres tâches de l'administration; les fonctionnaires semblaient avoir rempli ces formulaires avec un soin identique à celui apporté aux bons de charbons ou à la rentrée scolaire.'[39] The full horror of state attitudes to deportation is brought into sharp relief: the deportation of men, women and children is treated like any other administrative process, like award-ing ration cards or deciding on school return dates, while discussion of collaboration and deportation remain closed files, only to be opened when those in power deem it admissible. As Charles Forsdick argues, in *Meurtres pour mémoire*, memory is presented as subject to state interfer-ence so that the novel does not 'enact a straightforward unearthing [of the past]. Instead, it is ultimately a reflection on the mechanisms that prevent elements of the past from being exposed'.[40]

Yet, if the novel investigates the failure of the French state to acknowl-edge its role in past crimes, the novel also enacts a kind of reverse logic, for it is the systemising impulse of state institutions that allows Cadin to solve his crime. By contacting his former police academy colleague, Dalbois, he is given access to files on key figures in the case and valu-able information on the events of 17 October 1961, as well as a network of contacts and rare witnesses. He is also able to consult the records of the computerised municipal telephone system in Toulouse on the day of Bernard's murder, allowing him to identify the man (Veillut) whom the archivist, Lécusson, alerts to the young historian's interest in the wartime files. While the novel acknowledges that 'le système se protège efficace-ment … La police constitue l'un des éléments majeurs du dispositif',[41] a police inspector, police archives and municipal records are key to the resolution of the crime. In *Meurtres pour mémoire*, what can appear a to-talising state system is subverted from within so that a form of retributive justice has its day.

As with the other novels in this chapter, such representations of collaboration cannot be disentangled from the imperative to transmit the past. As in *Maudit Blood*, the primary vector for transmission is the parent-child relationship and this is seen to have failed with severe consequences for those born after the war. Bernard Thiraud, whose death triggers Cadin's investigation, is an orphan of sorts, a child brought up by his grandparents in the Parisian suburb of Drancy following his father's death on 17 October 1961 and whose mother has retreated into a form of voluntary mutism after witnessing her husband's assassination from their apartment window while heavily pregnant with Bernard. Carrying on his father's project of a short monograph on his home town of Drancy, Bernard stumbles across the wartime history of the Drancy transit camp and the culpability of Veillut who has the infamous distinction of having sent more Jewish children under three to the camp than any other regional administrator in France. Other damaged children of times of national conflicts are figured in the novel, such as the daughter of Marc Rosner, the police photographer who films the October 1961 demonstration. When Cadin meets her, Rosie is represented as having a pronounced speech impediment, an image of the partial and jumbled narrative of the past to have been passed on to succeeding generations.

However, if familial ties prove problematic in the narrative economy of the text other routes of memory are more resilient. There is, firstly, transmission via the work of historians. Father and son historians, Roger and Bernard Thiraud, and Claudine, Bernard's girlfriend, offer an academic circuit of memory. Cadin's reading of Roger's and Bernard's unfinished monograph on Drancy provides the final piece in the puzzle and is the catalyst for Cadin's disturbing dreamscape in which all narrative threads converge and links are made between 1942, 1961 and 1982. Secondly, transmission occurs via an investigative circuit as Cadin assembles documents, witness statements, film footage and telephone records to prove Veillut's guilt and reconstruct the story of his crimes. Thirdly, in a richly figurative sense, transmission occurs via metaphor and analogy as ghosts from the past haunt the present and memories of the Second World War intersect with those of the Algerian War in a powerful model of 'multidirectional memory'.[42]

In the opening scenes of the novel, a series of micro-narratives give the reader access to the viewpoints of two Algerian demonstrators and Roger Thiraud as they face the police repression of 17 October 1961. Their narrative perspective allows the victim's voice to frame the novel and humanises the statistics of horror which will characterise the sections devoted to the Jewish deportees later on. Indeed, Daeninckx's description of the police repression of 17 October 1961 is replete with markers of the occupation and a previous victimisation of a civilian population.[43] The French riot squad's march through the centre of Paris echoes the boots of the German occupying forces: 'le martèlement des bottes sur les pavés renforçait ce sentiment de fatalité'.[44] The arrested demonstrators, shocked and dazed, recall Jews rounded up by French policemen in the summer of 1942 to be transported by bus to the internment camp of Drancy: 'Cent, cent cinquante prisonniers. Pourtant, aucun d'eux ne songeait à s'enfuir, à libérer ses camarades. Paris était bouclé, toute fuite semblait d'avance vouée à l'échec'.[45] While the racist comments of witnesses resonate with wartime anti-Semitism: 'ils l'ont bien cherché, lui dit un passant. Roger Thiraud le fixa'.[46] A suggestive accretion of intra- and intertextual references bind 1942 and 1961 in the novel and set out the explosive potential of undetected pasts, once exposed, to detonate in the present and change the dominant narratives of collective memory. Like the importance of maps, modes of travel and public transport in *Meurtres pour mémoire*, new routes of memory are signposted by such multi-directional memory. They suggest that deviations are possible and that the past does not have to repeat itself in a closed circuit that prevents the flow of new information.

Meurtres pour mémoire sets out a different narrative patterning of collaboration to the preceding two novels. Daeninckx is focused less on the personal and political stakes of collaboration than on the mindset of the state functionary, efficient and capable and who implements inhuman directives in servile submission to his superiors. This form of collaboration could be termed *un crime de bureau* as Maurice Papon's actions would be labelled by some at his trial in 1997–98. Yet, the novel by no means exonerates such individuals and identifies them as contributing to the workings of governing elites whose systematising impulse has fatal consequences. More so than the other novels in this chapter, *Meurtres pour mémoire* emphasises the imperative of transmitting such a past to future generations, a process of transmission that makes visible 'complex processes of filiation' with other episodes in French history occluded by those in power.[47] For in Daeninckx's fictional universe, memories of the Second World War are generated and circulate in symbiosis with crimes from other distinct historical periods. Such memories are closely aligned to debates in the narrative present demonstrating the porosity between then and now, history and memory.

Conclusion

The crime fictions studied in this chapter highlight changes in the understanding of collaboration during the 1980s in three key respects. Firstly, they participate in a general move away from collaboration as individual aberration or personal failing towards an expansive notion of collaboration as a collective phenomenon. This is not to discount the persistence of certain tropes of collaboration from the late 1940s, such as the sexual connection between politics and personal choices, evident in *Collabo-Song*, or recourse to the metaphor of collaboration as disease or illness, signalled in *Maudit Blood*'s final reckoning with the Savetan clan and their family history of haemophilia. Yet, common to all three novels is a conception of collaboration as a multi-faceted phenomenon, a re-reading that has its roots in revisionist historical accounts of the extent and scope of collaboration in wartime France. Collaboration is not the minoritarian other of resistance in any of the fictions discussed here. Indeed, resistance could be said to stand as the great absence at the heart of all these fictions, glimpsed only tangentially and certainly not as a comforting moral choice with which to counterbalance the crimes of collaboration. In these crime fictions of the 1980s, the focus is upon the trajectories and actions of fictional collaborators whose life histories do not allow easy moral distinctions to be made between perpetrators and victims. In some instances drawn from real-life figures, these fictional protagonists accentuate the commingling of the fictional and the factual and the intense difficulty in making definitive judgements on the past

Secondly, all three crime fictions highlight the growing interest in a Jewish memory of the war years, a trend which would mark French cultural and political life into the 1990s. In all three novels, it is crimes against Jewish protagonists, individually or collectively, that drive the crime intrigue. Whether this is for economic gain and ideological reasons, as in *Maudit Blood*, self-interest and revenge, as in *Collabo-Song*, or due to careerism and indifference, as in *Meurtres pour mémoire*, collaboration and a deep history of French anti-Semitism cannot be untangled. In none of the novels do Jewish victims speak back; they are the dead, the unnamed or the maligned, the later the case for *Collabo-Song*'s Mireille/Rosette. Instead, it is for the reader to make empathic connections and to imagine Jewish wartime lives and destinies. In the decade of an obsession with a Jewish wartime memory as Henry Rousso terms it, it is this indictment of direct or indirect complicity in the persecution and deportation of Jews in France that convicts the fictive protagonists and constitutes the ethical charge of the novels.

Lastly, all three crime fictions set out the perils of non-transmission and the traumatising effects of suppressing the legacy of collaboration for individuals, families and national communities many decades later. The refusal to broach the legacies of collaboration is figured in *Maudit Blood* as a genetic time bomb that threatens to explode with each new generation of the Savetan family. In *Collabo-Song*, collaboration distorts family histories; sullies posthumous reputations and leads to misrepresentation of the past. In *Meurtres pour mémoire*, the secret of collaboration generates family breakdown, murder and state corruption as the past is buried to serve the needs of those in power. In none of the novels is any conventional form of justice enacted. While individuals may be made to pay for their crimes via arbitrary murder and execution, there is no sense that public acknowledgement will be undertaken or legal sanction imposed. Ultimately, the only strategy endorsed by all three novels is the importance of dialogue and discussion, memory work that, as Charles Forsdick suggests in relation to *Meurtres pour mémoire*, could replace passive knowledge of past events with active recognition.[48] Engaging with such troubled pasts does not necessarily mean being haunted by the crimes of collaboration. As all three novels infer, such engagement offers the possibility of breaking destructive cycles of remembrance and enabling successor generations to live with a past that can strengthen connection and solidarity in the present.

Notes

1   For an overview of this period, see Henry Rousso, *Le Syndrome de Vichy: de 1944 à nos jours* (Paris: Editions du Seuil, 1990), Chapter 1 'Le deuil inachevé', pp. 29–76.

2   These terms are taken from major studies of collaboration written during the 1970s and 1980s: Pascal Ory, *Les Collaborateurs 1940–1945* (Paris: Editions du Seuil, 1976), 'sujets tabous' (p. 7); Robert Paxton, *Vichy France: Old Guard and New Order 1940–1944* (New York: Columbia University Press, 1972), 'embarrassed silence' (p. xiii); Gerhard Hirschfeld and Patrick Marsh (eds), *Collaboration in France: Politics and Culture during the Nazi Occupation, 1940–1944* (Oxford: Berg, 1987), 'persistent reticence' (p. vii); and Bertram M. Gordon, *Collaborationism in France during the Second World War* (Ithaca, NY and London: Cornell University Press, 1980), 'sensitive subject' (p. 361).

3   Susan Suleiman, '"Choosing our past": Jean-Paul Sartre as memoirist of oc-
     cupied France', *Crises of Memory and the Second World War* (Cambridge,
     MA: Harvard University Press, 2006), pp. 13–35, analyses Sartre's three es-
     says on the occupation, published from August 1944 to August 1945. She
     highlights the silences of such articles on issues such as the ideological mo-
     tivations for collaboration and the virulent anti-Semitism of notorious col-
     laborators.
4   Jean-Paul Sartre, 'Qu'est-ce qu'un collaborateur?', *Situations III: lendemains
     de guerre* (Paris: Gallimard, 1976), pp. 43–61 (p. 46).
5   Sartre, 'Qu'est-ce qu'un collaborateur?', p. 58.
6   Michael Kelly, 'The view of collaboration during the "après-guerre"', in Hir-
     schfeld and Marsh (eds), *Collaboration in France*, pp. 239–51 (p. 243).
7   Kelly, 'The view of collaboration during the "après-guerre"', p. 244.
8   See Christopher Lloyd, *Uranus and la tête des autres* (Glasgow: University of
     Glasgow French and German Publications, 1994), for analysis of the novel
     and Aymé's wartime and post-war trajectory as writer and intellectual.
9   Audra L. Merfeld-Langston analyses the cultural politics of representing
     collaboration in Aymé's novel, *Uranus,* and its filmic adaptation by Claude
     Berri in 1990. She provides a comparative reading which argues for the
     complexity of collaboration's portrayal in Aymé's fiction and its more sani-
     tised depiction in Berri's film. See Audra L. Merfeld-Langston, 'From text
     to screen: portraits of collaboration in *Uranus*', *French Cultural Studies*, 21:3
     (2010), 178–91.
10   Paxton, *Vichy France*, p. xi.
11   Paxton, *Vichy France*, p. xiv.
12   Gerhard Hirschfeld, 'Collaboration in nazi-occupied France: some intro-
     ductory remarks', in Hirschfeld and Marsh (eds), *Collaboration in France*,
     pp. 1–14 (p. 7).
13   The film, although initially conceived as a project for the French public
     broadcasting channel ORTF, was first broadcast on French television in
     1981 after prolonged wrangling with the French authorities concerned by
     its overly negative portrayal of wartime France.
14   Alan Morris, *Collaboration and Resistance Reviewed: Writers and the Mode
     Rétro in Post-Gaullist France* (Oxford: Berg, 1992).
15   Morris, *Collaboration and Resistance Reviewed*, p. 82. A similar formula-
     tion, 'an orphaned generation', is used by Colin Nettelbeck in his examina-
     tion of post-war French war fiction, 'Getting the story right: narratives of
     the Second World War in post-1968 France', in Hirschfeld and Marsh (eds),
     Collaboration in France, pp. 252–93 (p. 275).
16   Critics, such as Nettelbeck and Morris, identify Modiano's early trilogy
     of occupation novels, *La Place de l'étoile* (1968), *La Ronde de nuit* (1969)
     and *Les Boulevards de ceinture* (1972) as a catalyst not only for literary

representation of the war years but also for new directions in historical research. Nettelbeck, in 'Getting the story right', labels Modiano a 'historical
visionary' (p. 285).

17   See Marie Chaix, *Les Lauriers du lac de Constance* (Paris: Editions du Seuil,
1974), Evelyne Le Garrec, *La Rive allemande de ma mémoire* (Paris: Editions
du Seuil, 1981), Pascal Jardin, *La Guerre à neuf ans* (Paris: Grasset, 1971),
Jean-Luc Maxence, *L'Ombre d'un père* (Paris: Editions Libres Hallier, 1978).

18   Nettelbeck, 'Getting the story right', p. 285.

19   See Alan Morris, 'From social outcasts to stars of the mainstream: the combatants of the collaboration in post-war France', *Journal of War and Culture
Studies*, 2:2 (2009), 167–79, for an analysis of changing representations of
French collaborators who fought for the Nazis in the post-war period. Morris discusses the contribution of the post-1980 *roman noir* to such representations, above all the work of Didier Daeninckx.

20   The novels and editions to be examined here are: Jean Mazarin, *Collabo-
Song* (Cadeilhan: Zulma, 1998); Georges-Jean Arnaud, *Maudit Blood* (Paris:
Editions du Rocher, 1998) and Didier Daeninckx, *Meurtres pour mémoire*
(Paris: Editions Gallimard, 1984).

21   I have taken this phrase from Henry Rousso's *Le Syndrome de Vichy*,
p. 153.

22   *Collabo-Song* won the Grand prix de littérature policière, in 1983. It has
been published twice, initially by Fleuve noir in 1981 and by Zulma in 1998.
Mazarin, writing as Emmanuel Errer, was to revisit the Second World War
in a number of novels, most notably *Un detour par l'enfer* (1987), the story
of a resistance hero who returns from the concentration camps to be shot
dead on 14 July at the foot of the local war memorial. The subsequent investigation uncovers substitution and subterfuge in a crime narrative that
offers a deconstruction of resistance heroism and its legitimacy in immediate post-war France.

23   As the title suggests, this 'collabo-song' is one that offers the reader melodic
variations on a theme, ending in a swansong of despair.

24   The phasing of collaboration in the novel has much in common with Stanley
Hoffman's staging of Vichy politics: from the ascendancy of the proponents
of the National Revolution, to the Vichy of the technocrats and, finally, the
emergence of Vichy as a police state. See *Decline or Renewal? France since
the 1930s* (New York: Viking Press, 1974), pp. 3–25.

25   Mazarin, *Collabo-Song*, p. 25 (a period in parentheses).

26   Mazarin, *Collabo-Song*, pp. 36–7 (he [Edouard] knew him to be anti-
Semitic, but no more so than many others in the profession).

27   Mazarin, *Collabo-Song*, p. 61. This is a reference to the round-up of non-
naturalised Jews in July 1942, the *rafle du Vélodrome d'Hiver*.

28   Mazarin, *Collabo-Song*, p. 12 (perhaps everything was not so black and
white).

29 Georges-Jean Arnaud has returned repeatedly to the war years in his volu-
minous body of work. Notable examples are: *L'Antizyklon des atroces* (1998)
which pivots on the present-day discovery of buried Zyklon B gas canis-
ters produced in the Beauvais region during the war years and destined for
the gas chambers. This crime intrigue is based on fact. *Spoliation* (2000)
revolves around the dispossession of Jews in wartime France when the
wealthy family of a former collaborator go to extreme lengths to keep secret
the provenance of their post-war fortune. *Maudit Blood* has been published
twice, initially under the name Georges Murey, *Maudit Blood* (Paris: Encre,
1985) and then under the name of Georges-Jean Arnaud in 1998.

30 Written in 1985, the novel is clearly influenced by debates on war crimes
and crimes against humanity rehearsed in the build-up to the trial of Klaus
Barbie in 1987. The reference to the possible prosecution of Maurice Papon
in the novel (p. 13) is revealing and indeed prophetic of what would occur.

31 Arnaud, *Maudit Blood*, p. 58 (Worse than a concentration camp, Auschwitz
at home in a pretty town like Toulouse, horror on the rue Alsace-Lorraine
with kapos as ferocious as those of the past).

32 Arnaud, *Maudit Blood*, p. 106 (As if after twenty years, a memory that pre-
ceded her birth had attached itself to her like a malignant tumour).

33 Arnaud, *Maudit Blood*, p. 234 (We killed the Jew out of greed but, above all,
in the beginning, from anachronistic Christian conviction. Executioners
were needed but executioners must also perish).

34 Arnaud, *Maudit Blood*, p. 234.

35 These editions are: Paris: Editions Gallimard, 1984, 1988, 1995, 1997, 1998,
1999, 2010; Editions Cercle Polar, 2001; Editions France Loisirs, 2002.

36 'Daeninckx, le Michelet de la série noire', *Le Matin,* 1985, dossier Didier
Daeninckx, Bibliothèque des littératures policières.

37 Daeninckx, *Meurtres pour mémoire*, p. 210. References in English will be to
Murder in Memoriam, trans. Liz Heron (London: Serpent's Tail, 1991),
p. 171; 'Not out of political conviction nor anti-Semitism, but just by obey-
ing the rules and carrying out the orders of the hierarchy'.

38 Daeninckx, *Meurtres pour mémoire*, pp. 63–4; 'DEforestation … DEmarca-
tion … DEfence … DEliberations of the special DElegation from Lanta',
Murder in Memoriam, p. 52.

39 Daeninckx, *Meurtres pour mémoire*, p. 64; 'DEportation was treated in ex-
actly the same way as other administrative tasks. The bureaucrats seem to
have filled in these forms with the same punctiliousness they brought to
coal coupons or the new school year', *Murder in Memoriam*, p. 52.

40 Charles Forsdick, '"Direction les oubliettes de l'histoire": witnessing the past
in the French polar', *French Cultural Studies*, 12:3 (2001), 333–50 (349).

41 Daeninckx, *Meurtres pour mémoire*, p. 135; 'The system has a good line
in self-protection. The police play a crucial role', *Murder in Memoriam*,
p. 110.

42 For a reading of the novel in this light, see Chapter 9, 'Hidden children: the ethics of multigenerational memory after 1961', in Michael Rothberg, *Multidirectional Memory: Remembering the Holocaust in the Age of Decolonization* (Palo Alto, CA: Stanford University Press, 2009), pp. 266–308.

43 Cadin describes the 17 October 1961 as 'un Oradour en plein Paris', *Meurtres pour mémoire*, p. 81; 'an Oradour massacre in the middle of Paris', *Murder in Memoriam*, p. 67, referring to the massacre of French civilians in the village of Oradour in 1944 by the German division Das Reich as they fled France ahead of the Allied invasion.

44 Daeninckx, *Meurtres pour mémoire*, p. 30; 'the hammering of boots on cobblestones reinforced this sense of doom', *Murder in Memoriam*, p. 24.

45 Daeninckx, *Meurtres pour mémoire*, p. 106; 'A hundred, a hundred and fifty prisoners. Yet none of them thought of escaping or freeing their comrades. Paris was caged in, all flight seemed doomed to failure', *Murder in Memoriam*, pp. 87–8.

46 Daeninckx, *Meurtres pour mémoire*, p. 34; 'They were asking for it, said a passer-by. Roger stared at him', *Murder in Memoriam*, p. 27.

47 Forsdick, 'Direction les oubliettes de l'histoire', p. 344.

48 Forsdick, 'Direction les oubliettes de l'histoire', pp. 349–50.

4

Survivor stories: representing persecution and extermination in French crime fiction of the 1980s and 1990s

The 1980s and 1990s witnessed an acceleration of interest in memories of the Second World War as those who had experienced such events began to disappear. These were years of a relay of memory, the transmission of war memories from a survivor generation to successor generations, as lived memory moved into the realm of cultural memory. However, this process of transmission was one fraught with difficulties and marked by the urgency to capture and preserve such war memories. The survivor stories which emerged in these decades were, therefore, charged narratives. They were stories which conformed to existing narrative templates for understanding the war years (victimisation and heroism) but also challenged such constructions of the past evoking the moral ambiguities of wartime memories and their legacies. They were also mobilised as potent stories in the context of present-day debates over collective guilt and responsibility, above all in relation to the Final Solution and the role of nations and peoples beyond Nazi Germany. The 1980s and 1990s were, therefore, decades which highlighted the fact that 'memory is a battlefield, where nothing is neutral and where everything is continually contested'.[1]

This chapter will read selected French crime fictions against such a backdrop, focusing on the figure of the survivor and representations of persecution and extermination. It will begin by setting out the general context of the 1980s and 1990s and will map out the coordinates of European and North-American re-engagement with memories of the Second World War. For with the increasing historicisation of the war years came reinterpretation and reappraisal as war stories were made to speak to contemporary concerns, igniting debate and controversy. It will then proceed to examine the specific case of France, above all reawakened memories of the deportation of Jews from France and the complicity of the Vichy regime. The chapter will then discuss novels by three crime writers: Gérard Delteil, Thierry Jonquet and Konop. All three novelists are representative of a renewed impetus in French crime fiction of these years to confront memories of the Second World War, over forty years after events. Their novels investigate the processes involved in transmitting war memories from one generation to the next and the impact of survivor stories on successor generations. They interrogate received views of the concentration camps and their legacies. Equally, these fictions highlight the difficulties involved in integrating survivor stories into broader considerations of guilt, responsibility and justice. Such novels can be read as demonstrating, in literary form, the changing contours of a French memorial landscape of the Second World War.

A memory boom

The 1980s and 1990s witnessed a resurgence of public interest in memories of the Second World War in Europe and elsewhere. This can be attributed to three main developments. Firstly, memories of the Second World War gained prominence due to the extraordinary media profile accorded anniversary commemorations marking significant events of the period 1939–45: from the fortieth and fiftieth anniversaries of the Battle of Britain and Dunkirk to the official state ceremonies marking D-Day in 1984 and 1994, VE and VJ Day in 1985 and 1995 and the liberation of the concentration camps, particularly Auschwitz. These events, broadcast to a receptive global audience, called upon individuals and national communities to register the presence of the past in their own lives and to reflect on their relationship to such formative collective experiences. Such commemorations provided the opportunity to celebrate narratives of national fortitude and suffering (the heroism of resistance and liberation) and to reinforce present-day initiatives aimed at international reconciliation and cooperation. They also served as a flashpoint for debates on the politics of memory: whose war experiences were being remembered, how and by whom?[2]

Secondly, public interest in the Second World War increased in response to historical reassessments of the Holocaust as mass murder on an unprecedented scale. In the cultural sphere, the establishment of new museums and audio-visual archives and the success of fictional and documentary films, such as Stephen Spielberg's *Schindler's List* (1993), contributed to a recasting of the Holocaust as the defining event of twentieth-century history and one which demanded public reflection and engagement. As Annette Wieviorka argues, the 1980s ushered in the era of the witness, when the Holocaust survivor moved from the sphere of 'individual memory inscribed in a closed ethnic group, and constructed in terms of family stories' to take up the role of witness, called upon to answer a social demand for testimony that could serve a pedagogical purpose.[3] Within the context of the courtroom, above all the trials of former Nazi war criminals or those tried for complicity in crimes against humanity, the Holocaust witness emerged as 'the existential witness, the man of memory who embodies the past and demonstrates that it is present still'.[4] As the custodian of the past, the Holocaust survivor-witness would come to symbolise the urgency of a duty to remember and the value of testimony for future generations.

The third factor to play an important part in the renewal of interest in the Second World War in these decades was the ending of the Cold War and the collapse of the Soviet Union. This geo-political realignment brought to the surface new perspectives on the war years as archives opened in the former communist states and individual memories, which had not been admissible under the previous regime, were publicly aired, often for the first time. Such individual memories offered an arena of potential criticism outside state-sponsored control and revealed the persistence of survivor stories which did not fit predetermined ideological schemas. Indeed, for Luisa Passerini, in her reading of the Italian context, what occurred post-1989 more generally was a greater receptivity to new aspects of past happenings. These 'delayed memories' of the recent past had a galvanising effect as: 'Fifty years on from the end of resistance to Nazism/fascism, it is clear that a great deal of the whole period has not been remembered publicly or recorded as history.'[5]

Reawakened memories

This global reconfiguration of war memories impacted upon French memories, albeit coloured by the distinctive experiences of France as an occupied country with a war record of collaboration, resistance and bloody liberation. Firstly, France, like its European and North-American counterparts, witnessed a reawakening of Jewish memory. This reawakened memory was generated partly by external factors, such as the crisis surrounding the Six-Day War in 1967 and its effects on the French-Jewish community; the role of American-Jewish organisations in promoting awareness of the Holocaust, and the impact of film and television, such as the American mini-series *Holocaust*, broadcast in France in 1979 and widely acknowledged to have reopened public debate on the legacies of the Holocaust.[6] Within France itself, the growing disquiet at the publication of articles and studies promoting Holocaust denial, as well as the provocative pronouncements and political ascendancy of the extreme right in the 1980s, specifically Jean-Marie Le Pen's Front National, fuelled fears that France had yet to confront a deep history of indigenous anti-Semitism.[7] Committed to the project of educating the wider public about the Holocaust, both survivors and the French historical community had to accept the fact that with the transmission of such war memories came opportunities for a network of Holocaust deniers to insinuate themselves into legitimate debates.[8]

The second major shift in French public consciousness of the war years in these decades was the emphasis on the role of the Vichy regime in the deportation of Jews from France. As Joan B. Wolf comments, in these years, the Holocaust, as an episode of mass suffering aided and abetted by the French authorities, 'served as a theater for various scripts about national identity', above all those relating to wartime collaboration and French guilt.[9] Rather than focus on the specificity of the Jewish genocide itself, the reinvestigation of the past in a French context grappled with the legacy of Vichy, a regime which had purported to safeguard French interests – the shield protecting France from the worst incursions of German rule – but which was increasingly cast as the perpetrator of human rights abuses. As Wolf notes, during the late 1980s and early 1990s, a narrative evolved which made a distinction between the France *of* Vichy and the French *under* Vichy, the latter the unwitting victims of a regime which had ruled in name alone.[10] As the fiftieth anniversary commemorations reached their nadir in France in the early 1990s, it was the role of the Vichy regime and the Parisian police authorities in the *rafle du Vélodrome d'Hiver*, the round-up of nearly 13,000 Jewish men, women and children on the night of 16/17 July 1942, that gripped public opinion. It generated a campaign for greater public recognition of the role of the French state and its agents in such coordinated persecution.[11] The stakes and symbolism of such national recognition were raised yet further by the third feature of French public engagement with the war years in these decades: the recourse to the courtroom and trials for crimes against humanity.

If the 1980s and the 1990s can be described as the era of the witness, nowhere was this phenomenon more evident than in France. From the late 1970s to the late 1990s, the French courtroom became an arena of memory, charged not only with judging the crimes and misdemeanours of leading German and French functionaries and war criminals but also with yielding lessons on the past and offering testimony which would serve a symbolic function. While a number of leading Vichy figures had been charged and convicted of war crimes in the early 1950s, it was the prosecution of crimes against humanity which enabled the French legal system to pursue individuals many years later as, from December 1964, the French National Assembly voted to abolish the statute of limitations for such crimes and incorporated this category of offence into French law.[12] Crimes against humanity were defined as 'murder, extermination, enslavement, deportation, and other inhumane acts committed against any civilian population, before or during the war, or persecutions on political, racial or religious grounds'.[13] Such laws were voted in with the prosecution of Nazi war criminals in mind, such as Klaus Barbie, Head of the Gestapo in Lyon, 1942–44, tried in France in 1987. Yet, by the early 1980s, legal processes had gathered momentum to indict leading Vichy officials Jean Leguay, René Bousquet and Maurice Papon, as well as regional militia leader, Paul Touvier, for crimes against humanity.[14] While Leguay and Bousquet were never to reach the courtroom, the trials of Paul Touvier and Maurice Papon in the 1990s were promoted as events of national importance that promised a salutary encounter with France's Vichy past. However, the trials exposed the historical and moral difficulties inherent in revisiting the past many years later.

Firstly, both trials demonstrated the mismatch between the legal process and historical research as interpretative frames for investigating the past. The requirements of the court to come to clear-cut judgments on individual actions and intentions in the past clashed with the intellectual modality of the historians called to testify. Their working methods, predicated on hypothetical analysis and conjecture, meant that they could not make definitive judgments when put in the witness box. As leading French historians asserted, the trials revealed a fundamental incompatibility between the legal context and historical record that could not be bridged without contortion of the historical evidence on the one hand and legal process on the other.[15] Secondly, the two trials accentuated the moral dilemmas involved in judging events and motivations more than fifty years later. Key to such debates was the probable knowledge that Vichy functionaries, such as Maurice Papon, could have had of the final destination of the Jewish people whose deportation orders they signed. While prosecuting lawyers and witnesses debated what could be inferred from the contextual information available, it was impossible to assert definitively what Papon knew of the wider mechanisms of the Holocaust.

Indeed, as Nancy Wood has noted, it was not so much a question of the limits of knowledge as a more profoundly personal and philosophical dilemma that 'apprehension of the Final Solution was ultimately something upon which neither law not history could – or should – make confident pronouncements'.[16] Knowing was not necessarily synonymous with cognition of the enormity of events and the ideological system in which they were embedded.

If, from the perspective of historical community, assessment of the trials was hedged with caveats and reservations, the pre-eminence accorded the survivors and their testimony was one outcome which many commentators looked to with greater optimism. For many who testified, it was the first time that they had felt a public sense of justice was being rendered not only to them but also to those who had either disappeared during the war years or died since. In this context, the courtroom gave a platform to witness testimony which promised public legitimacy and the opportunity to bear witness in a personal sense that offered 'a release from survivorship'.[17] Such aspirations were not always realised on cross-examination as the demands for factual certainties and causal connections exposed the limits of individual knowledge and understanding. But it was the presence of memory people, such as Simone Lagrange during the Barbie trial, and the intimacy created by the staging of their personal tragedy in court that would be remembered by many who watched televised footage of the trials or read the daily reporting.[18] In response, the figure of the survivor-witness, as the carrier of memory for a nation, would become one of the privileged tropes in popular fiction of these decades.

Survivor stories: crime, guilt and responsibility

During the 1980s and 1990s, a significant number of French crime novels were published structured around the revelation of criminal secrets from the war years and their disruptive effects on the narrative present.[19] On one level, this thematic trend is unsurprising given the context of the 1980s and 1990s and the visibility of the French courtroom as a privileged *lieu de mémoire*, legitimising the public airing of questions of guilt and responsibility, justice and reparation. Yet, these were also decades which marked a shift in perspective for French crime fiction and its representation of the war years in two key respects. Firstly, French crime novels about the Second World War in these years were more likely than their predecessors to be built upon extensive historical research, combining

scholarly investigation with imaginative construction. Such an engagement with historical materials from the war years can be attributed to
generational change, as French crime writers born during or after the
war years approached the period with no personal memory of events
and a marked sense of the ethical stakes involved in writing about such a
period in the age of Holocaust denial.[20] A second feature of these crime
fictions was the tendency to centre investigations on the French justice
system itself, thereby framing war memories in term of legal redress, restitution and a search for responsibility and accountability. Moving beyond
the family-centric narratives of Jewish persecution examined in Chapter
2, the novels of the 1980s and 1990s embraced a new cast of characters
drawn from the institutions that were subject to public scrutiny in the
trials for crimes against humanity: police inspectors (Jewish and non-
Jewish), examining judges and German and French civil servants. Key to
such a recasting of war memory was the figure of the Holocaust survivor
and the fraught passage from silence to testimony. In many crime novels
of these decades, it was the resurfacing of the war memories of the survivor-witness which generated narrative momentum. Such silenced war
memories, resurgent in the present, allowed for reinterpretations of the
past that defied traditional narrative templates of war and occupation.
These hybrid crime fictions – at once historical investigation and creative
reconstruction – offer, therefore, rich material for examining the role of
popular fiction in the encounters between public history and personal
memory in the changing landscape of post-war French memory. It is to
three examples of these hybrid crime fictions that this chapter will now
turn.

Gérard Delteil's *KZ retour vers l'enfer* (1987), Thierry Jonquet's *Les
Orpailleurs* (1993) and Konop's *Pas de kaddish pour Sylberstein* (1993)
are all crime fictions which engage explicitly with survivor stories and
probe questions of crime, guilt and responsibility.[21] All feature fictional
protagonists who have experienced life in the concentration camps or
have perpetrated mass persecution and extermination. These stories are
investigated by younger characters who, in a professional capacity (as a
journalist, judge and police inspector), face the ethical dilemma of how
to integrate such traumatic memories into broader juridical frameworks
relating to crime, perpetration and justice. In discussing these three novels in their socio-historical context, this chapter will ask the following
questions: firstly, how is the figure of the survivor depicted and how is
his testimony represented? Discussion here will focus on the listeners to
such stories and how they respond to what Dori Laub calls the 'cultural

shock value' of the Holocaust as an event which has yet to be assimilated fully into public consciousness.[22] It will be argued that these fictional interlocutors reflect on popular perceptions of successor generations and their relationship to the past. Secondly, how do these texts represent persecution and extermination? The emphasis will be on how and to what extent these novels rework common narratives of the concentration camps and their legacy. Lastly, how do these texts address questions of individual and collective guilt and responsibility? The courtroom context of the 1990s highlighted the opportunities but also the pitfalls of attempting to judge degrees of participation, complicity and knowledge of the Holocaust many years later. All the novels discussed here pose troubling questions of French, and more broadly European, collusion in the events of the Holocaust. Ultimately, this chapter will argue that the novels of crime writers, such as Delteil, Jonquet and Konop, represent a refusal to 'turn the page on the past'. They champion the need for a 'critical self-reflection' on the war and challenge the reader to speculate on their own responses to such survivor stories in the present.[23]

Gérard Delteil's *KZ retour vers l'enfer* revolves around the war memories of concentration camp survivor, Paul Liebman, who is saved from a racist attack on the Parisian metro one evening in 1984 by an unnamed journalist. The journalist, born in 1942 (and therefore importantly of the successor generation), strikes up a friendship with Liebman in the narrative present and triggers Liebman's desire to give a testimonial account of his life as René Maillard, a Jewish resister deported to an unspecified concentration camp.[24] The aim of the sequences of interviews is for the journalist to write a general account which would enable Liebman/ Maillard's story to be fully known. However, as the narrative progresses, what appears a faithful attempt to record the survivor's story for posterity becomes undermined and the competing emotional needs of the survivor-witness and the listener come to colour the testimonial project. For while Liebman has testified at the early post-war trials of SS officers out of a sense of duty towards those who did not survive, the interviews with the journalist-narrator generate feelings of guilt, betrayal and grief which reveal how trapped in the past he remains. This is evident primarily in the form of the novel which alternates between a textual present, 1984, and a reconstructed past, Poland in 1944. From the typographical presentation of the novel, it is the textual present which would appear to be the parenthetical time frame, identified by italicised script. It is little more than a framing device for Liebman/Maillard's concentration camp account until the epilogue where the two time frames merge. In one sense, therefore, the text signals the extent to which the survivor-witness is a prisoner of his past.

It is the privileged relationship with an empathic listener which enables the release of testimony. As Dori Laub has discussed, the testimony of a traumatic event can only come into being in the presence of a listener, one who agrees to act as 'a participant, and a co-owner of the traumatic event'.[25] In the absence of such interpersonal investment, no process of transmission can take place and the witness cannot escape the memory of the event, in this case the Holocaust, which has ended but continues to colour her or his post-war life. In *KZ*, the unnamed journalist fulfils the function of guide and companion on Liebman/Maillard's journey into the past, both psychologically in his transcription of events – which is what we as readers access – and literally as he revisits the site of the camp in order to unearth treasure which Liebman/Maillard claims is hidden there. Yet as the unnamed journalist discovers, Liebman/Maillard's testimony is littered with silences and omissions. Did he serve as an informant for the Gestapo in the camp after his torture and the threat that his sister would be forced into the camp brothel? Was he involved, inadvertently, in the failure of the camp uprising in which all are killed but him? Did he know that the camp archives (and not treasure) which the journalist-narrator unearths would exonerate or condemn him? The impact of the testimony on the journalist-narrator is signalled in the epilogue to the text as he tracks down the camp Gestapo officer who tortured and black-mailed Liebman/Maillard, Kaltenbrunner, now in retirement in Austria, and executes him with a bullet to the back of the head. The novel ends with murder and a delayed form of retribution carried out in memory of the dead.

In many ways, the shock, anger and merciless retribution of the journalist-narrator are responses sanctioned by the depiction of the concentration camps in the novel. The conventional binary oppositions of perpetrator/victim, German/Jew, SS/deportee are overturned in the novel and demonstrate Delteil's debt to actual witness accounts, such as those of political deportee and concentration camp survivor David Rousset whom Delteil acknowledges in his bibliography.[26] For, as in Rousset's hybrid texts, part autobiography, part historical chronicle, *KZ* focuses upon the complicity and suffering that bound and divided deportees and structured their relations with the SS guards, the civilian soldiers and the workers who toiled alongside them in the industrial complex that adjoins this fictional camp.[27] In *KZ, kapos* (prisoner leaders) are depicted as exploiting relations with both political and common-law deportees and operating lucrative deals with the SS officers who are presented as greedy hypocrites, some intoxicated with the power to control life and death in the camp, most anxious to avoid being sent to the Eastern Front and almost certain death in late 1944. The SS corps itself is presented as divided by power struggles as the concern to increase industrial production for the war effort clashes with internal security measures taken to prevent information from the camp being leaked to advancing Soviet troops. Yet, throughout, Delteil remains committed to the political deportees, above all those in the international committee who plot and execute the failed camp uprising. This grouping is credited with a dignity and a courage that make them the novel's heroes, although doomed to die at the hands of superior forces. Such a presentation makes Liebman/Maillard's moral dilemma over his real or inadvertent role in the crushing of the revolt more poignant for, as the journalist-narrator recognises: '... les choses se révélaient si complexes, si peu conformes à toutes sortes de schémas reçus ... '.[28]

It is this fracturing of received narratives of the concentration camps that preoccupies the journalist-narrator and leads to the bloody denouement of murder and revenge. One of the innovations of the novel is to look beyond the cultural clichés of war (German guards versus camp inmates) and to consider degrees of collective guilt and responsibility beyond the parameters of the concentration camp. In *KZ*, this expansive framing converges on the figure of the onlooker or bystander to the Holocaust, those like the Polish villagers who live near the concentration camp and profit from the suffering of others. This indictment of the bystander is, firstly, represented when Liebman/Maillard is sent on a reconnaissance mission to map out the terrain around the camp in preparation for the imminent camp uprising. What he sees in the village a short distance from the camp are the easy relations of the Germans and the Polish villagers, including the sale of ashes from the crematoria as fertiliser for the land of the local farmers. This abuse of the deportees is reinforced by the narrator's insistence on the indigenous anti-Semitism of the surrounding villagers, such that when two SS officers and a collaborating *kapo* escape during the camp uprising with looted goods, they are murdered as Jews. The ignorant and stereotypical depiction of them by the Polish villagers who find them wandering the woods – 'ils ont l'odeur caractéristique du Juif et celui-là en a bien la tête' – underscores not only their complicity with the SS but the sharing of deep-rooted ethnic prejudices given free rein during the occupation.[29] This construction of the local Polish villagers as willing accomplices to the German occupier is reiterated in the narrative present on the site of the obliterated unnamed camp when the journalist-narrator meets a young Polish student. Despite evidence to the contrary, the young student is unwilling to accept any narrative of responsibility which implies collusion in the Holocaust and reaffirms a war story of Polish victimisation.

In a similar vein, the journalist-narrator's journeys through present-day West Germany in the novel's epilogue gesture at a nation's inability to grasp its historical role as a society complicit in mass persecution and extermination. As he travels the *autobahn*, the journalist-narrator specu-lates on the likely knowledge the wealthy families he views have of the conditions of its construction: 'le splendide autobahn que nous parcourions ensemble avait été réalisé par une main d'oeuvre concentrationnaire – le transport des énormes blocs de soubassements avait coûté la vie à des milliers d'esclaves au crâne rasé'.[30] Indeed, the comfortable post-war lives of many of the major SS figures from the unnamed concentration camp of Liebman/Maillard's testimony indicate that, as a community, Germany has in no way mastered it past. The journalist-narrator meets a selection of successful businessmen and politicians who have either continued their racist views under a different guise, in this case campaigns against immigrants, or who have benefited from the protection of the wider community. The journalist-narrator soon learns that an implacable si-lence prevents any meaningful dialogue on the wartime past, smothering individual or collective reckonings with the crimes of Nazism.

As a novel of the late 1980s, *KZ* is indicative of broader popular un-derstandings of the processes involved in transmitting war memories from one generation to the next. Coming to testimony in this novel is fraught with dangers and pitfalls, both for the survivor-witness and for the empathic listener, the journalist-narrator whose final act of violence suggests an inability to integrate the past into the present. In parallel, *KZ* offers a morally ambiguous representation of the concentration camps that throws off kilter Manichaean images of self and other, victim and perpetrator, as prisoners collude in and profit from fellow deportees' suf-fering. However, it is the framing of such a fictionalised testimony within a larger European context of collective guilt and responsibility which of-fers the most intriguing remodelling of war memory. This is a model which traverses national borders and calls into question purely German responsibility for the Holocaust in order to point a finger at the collusion of local communities, such as the Polish villagers of the text, and the si-lences of West German society. What is equally striking for readers today is the fact that this remodelling of collective guilt and responsibility in the late 1980s makes no reference to French complicity and responsibility. By the early 1990s, the prominence of debates concerning Vichy's culpability in the Holocaust would make such an omission difficult to sustain. By then, the implications of French participation in the mechanisms of the Holocaust had become a major focus of French memory campaigners. These are exploited to dramatic effect by the remaining two crime writers in this chapter.

Thierry Jonquet's *Les Orpailleurs* (1993) concerns the murder of four women, each left to bleed to death after having her right hand severed off and left at the crime scene.[31] A young examining judge, Nadia Lintz, is assigned the investigation of these signature crimes, taking her on a journey back in time to the war years and across Europe to Auschwitz-Birkenau, the primary crime scene to which all the murders are linked. Unlike *KZ*, *Les Orpailleurs* does not present survivor testimony as a continuous narrative, emerging fully formed into the narrative present. Rather, the life histories and testimonies of two survivors are presented in fragments and connected to key objects, in this case a ruby-red ring which functions as a memorial cue, triggering the bloody murders in the present. The primary narrative frame for transmission of the survivor's story is the legal process. It is Nadia Lintz, the examining judge, who accumulates material evidence of the past and to whom Holocaust survivor Isy Szalcman tells his story and that of the murderer, Maurice Rosenfeld, both marked by the wartime past and personal loss.

The first representation of the survivor comes via case notes and a legal history. Lintz discovers Szalcman's past when she speaks to a retired lawyer who defended Szalcman in the early 1950s against a charge of armed robbery. As Montagnac recounts his defence strategy, he evokes Szalcman's past as a fourteen-year-old displaced person, a teenage survivor of Auschwitz and Buchenwald, following the extermination of his family in Poland. For Montagnac, Szalcman is emblematic of a community of Holocaust survivors who have remained trapped in the unending present of the concentration camps, unable to reconcile such traumatic events with identity in the present: 'Oui c'est cela, tout se passait comme s'il n'était jamais sorti du camp. Il y avait cette vie qui s'écoulait, jour après jour, ici, parmi nous, une vie factice en vérité, tandis que l'autre, la vraie, continuait "là-bas" ...'.[32] As in *KZ*, Lintz offers Szalcman an empathic listener for his concentrationary memories and a means of escaping entrapment in the past. As an examining judge, trained to listen to witness statements and depositions, she is well placed to understand the nuances and silences of testimony, as well as the emotional needs of her interlocutor. However, *Les Orpailleurs* situates such a professional framing of Holocaust testimony against the personal history of the listener, in this case a family connection to wartime anti-Semitism. For it transpires that Lintz's father was active during the occupation as a collaborator who profited from the pillaging of Jewish apartments, using such accumulated wealth to make a successful post-war career for himself as a businessman. The relationship of the listener to the survivor is not, therefore, without emotional baggage. Indeed, the novel implies that Lintz's ethical commitment to listen to the testimony of the Holocaust survivor is built upon a personal inability to hear a story of French guilt and responsibility much closer to home.

The second representation of the survivor comes in the character of Maurice Rosenfeld whose murderous rage at the wartime loss of his fiancée, Marie, triggers crimes in the present. Maurice gives Marie a family heirloom, a ruby-red ring, just before she is rounded up and deported to the extermination camps. It is this ring which condemns a series of young women to death as Maurice attempts to retrace its journey of ownership from France to Poland in the forlorn hope of locating Marie. As a survivor-witness, Rosenfeld might be described as an example of what Tzvetan Todorov has called a *mémoire littérale* of the past. In this model, memories of a traumatic past are retained in a literal form.[33] They come to define all moments of existence and subjugate the past to the present in ways which prevent any liberation from trauma. Rosenfeld's obsessive killings suggest this formulation of the Holocaust as unassimilated memory and one which takes symbolic form in the ruby-red ring justifying, in the mind of the survivor, unconscionable acts. In contrast, the figure of Isy Szalcman suggests an alternative model for the survivor-witness, one who represents the value of a *mémoire exemplaire*. In this use of memory, the past becomes a means of understanding analogous situations in the present and offers a platform for action. Testimony opens up the possibility for the survivor-witness to take ownership of their trauma. By refusing immersion in the past and privileging the process of transmission, Szalcman offers a critical perspective on the Holocaust which can be handed down to successor generations. It is this exemplary approach to memory work and dialogue which emerges in the novel as a key strategy in grappling with the legacies of the concentration camps.

In *Les Orpailleurs*, the legacies of the concentration camps are made evident in the family histories of the main protagonists, in the fragmented and disturbed obsession of the killer and in the representation of the sites of atrocity themselves. The geographical locations of the novel deliberately imitate routes of deportation as the main protagonists travel from France to Germany and then Poland in a symbolic identification with the victims of enforced exile. Yet, in Poland, as the narrative makes clear, competing versions of the Holocaust connect to a troubling politics of memory. This is evident in the contrasting representations of the sites of Auschwitz and Birkenau, both part of the industrial complex that made up the concentration camp and its adjoining factories. Lintz's initial visit to Auschwitz offers a vision of the commodification of memory. The camp is described as having been turned into a museum, replete with advertising hoardings, guidebook, gift shop and a memorial circuit that is packaged for tourists and their cameras. Here, the novel suggests, there is no sustained effort to induce critical reflection on the Holocaust but rather a sanitised re-presentation of the past that is acceptable to all. In sharp counterpoint, Lintz's visit to Birkenau in the company of Szalcman is one marked by a confrontation with neglected war memories: 'Elle [Lintz] se souvint du musée d'Auschwitz, si soigneusement entretenu, si jalousement gardé. Birkenau ressemblait à un terrain vague, un dépotoir du souvenir'.[34] Birkenau is the 'rubbish heap of memory', a memorial site that has been abandoned unlike the controlled and policed memory of Auschwitz. It is Szalcman, the survivor-witness, who brings such neglected wartime memories back to life for Lintz as he guides her around the crumbling camp buildings, identifying significant landmarks, such as the ramp on which the initial selections of deportees were made. Like the survivor-witness of *KZ*, what he has to tell is not a story of unmitigated suffering. As he acknowledges, his relative privilege as a deportee who worked in the Canada barracks gave him a greater chance of survival.[35] This morally ambiguous narrative undermines the victim status of the deportee associated with the Auschwitz museum in the novel. It also opens up the possibility of addressing questions of collective guilt and culpability which go beyond the conventional portrayal of the German as perpetrator and lead to a disturbing representation of complicity and collusion in past and present-day Poland and France.

Les Orpailleurs stages the complex international and transhistorical connections thrown up by the Holocaust. The novel begins in Paris and is built upon the premise that murder in the present is connected to questions of who knew what, when and how in the past, above all in relation to the Holocaust. For the novel creates a series of analogies between the deportation of Jews during the Second World War and crimes in the present. The latter relate both to the pathological killings of Rosenfeld and an illegal meat trade which begins in Poland to end in France as inedible meat is transported to Paris for sale. The rotten meat, discovered in a warehouse in Paris, stands in for the convoys of human beings sent in the opposite direction to Poland during the war years and whose butchery in the concentration camps is re-enacted on the female victims of the novel, all mutilated and left to bleed to death in present-day Paris. These women – three Polish victims and one French victim – represent, in graphic form, the interpenetration of French and Polish war memories and the diffuse circuits of knowledge, complicity and crime which reverberate in the present.

In terms of collective guilt and responsibility, *Les Orpailleurs* evacuates any reference to German figures and focuses, like *KZ*, on the complacency of onlookers and bystanders, above all the local Polish community who live near the Auschwitz complex. In the aftermath of war, the local people of Plaswy dig up the area around the extermination camp in search of valuable items to be retained as mementoes or sold on for profit. It is via this circuit of Holocaust memorabilia that Marie's ring is identified on the hand of the first French victim of the novel, condemning her to death. As a mobile carrier of memory, the ring stands in for this trade in human misery, for it is when Lintz eventually tracks down the ring to its origin in Plaswy that she is confronted with a narrative of indifference and crass exploitation of the Jewish victims of the camp. As her counterpart, Polish police inspector Sosnowski, confesses such a post-war traffic in Jewish possessions was 'un secret de polichinelle', an open secret widely known and condoned in the region.[36] Those who lived nearby the extermination camp knew its purpose and were willing to profit from such misery for personal gain: 'vous vous trouvez dans le plus grand cimetière du monde! Il n'y pas une seule motte de terre, pas une seule, vous entendez, qui ne renferme des cendres humaines! Des millions, des millions de cadavres … brûlés, enterrés sous cette herbe si tendre! On apercevait les flammes des crématoires à plus de vingt kilomètres à la ronde!'[37] Yet, as the text itself confirms, wilful collusion in mass persecution and extermination was not a uniquely Polish phenomenon. The collaboration of Lintz's own father in France, and her belated discovery that her much loved piano was pillaged from a Jewish home during the war, demonstrate that such 'open secrets' of profiteering and anti-Semitism traverse national borders in a vast network of collective guilt and responsibility.

The novel ends with the transmission of war memories from one generation to the next as Szalcman passes on his survivor story to Lintz while they walk through the dilapidated site of Birkenau. By bequeathing her the ruby-red ring, Szalcman also confers upon her the role of guardian of memory and the social imperative to remember. In *Les Orpailleurs*, the reader too is challenged to confront the complex filiations of wartime memory and to reflect upon the reverberations of the past in the present. From the butchery of young women in the textual present to the mass murder of Jewish families in the past, the novel speculates on the extent to which wartime persecution and extermination have impacted upon the present and generated appropriate forms of remembrance. Should we remember the Holocaust in the monumentalising project of the Auschwitz camp museum and run the risk of petrifying the past via an injunction to remember? Should we adopt the more provisional and personal memory work symbolised by the survivor-witness Szalcman and his individual story of survival? The concentration camps and the Holocaust are unfinished business, the novel suggests, for both survivors and successor generations and it is only through intergenerational dialogue that a form of understanding can be reached.

It is this notion of intergenerational and transnational dialogue on the past which structures the investigation of memories of persecution and extermination in the final text in this chapter, Konop's *Pas de kaddish pour Sylberstein* (1993) The innovation of Konop's crime narrative is to set the investigation of the wartime past within the Jewish community itself as Samuel Benamou, a Jewish police inspector in the Belleville district of Paris, attempts to unravel the motivation behind the murder of a German tourist by an orthodox Jew and antique dealer, Sylberstein, on 16 July 1992. As the date of the crime suggests, this novel explicitly connects transgression in the present to national debates on the commemoration of the *rafle du Vélodrome d'Hiver* of 16/17 July 1942, a hot topic on the fiftieth anniversary of events in 1992. However, in a series of narrative twists and turns, the novel ends by focusing on a different set of war memories. These relate to the rehabilitation of SS officers at the war's end as leading political activists in the new East German state and the search for a notorious Ukrainian war criminal, Kravéniouk, who has reinvented himself as none other than Sylberstein.

The figure of the survivor-witness in the novel is a complex and problematic one. Sylberstein/Kravéniouk provides false testimony, claiming to have killed Rudi Stoltz, the German tourist in his antiques shop, after recognising him as an SS officer who massacred Jews in his home village of Chmertzov in 1944.[38] Benamou acts as the successor generation's empathic listener as he takes Sylberstein/Kravéniouk's legal deposition and resigns from the police force in a gesture of protest as he registers the symbolic date of the murder. Sylberstein/Kravéniouk's death from natural causes in custody a few months later reinforces a sense of the fateful return of the past and the injustices of French state responses to such persecution. His personal investigation is, therefore, both a personal homage to a survivor-witness and an attempt to assuage his own guilt by association as a member of the Parisian police force whom he knows to have been active in the *rafle du Vélodrome d'Hiver*. In interviewing a series of figures from Sylberstein's past and that of the victim, Stoltz, Benamou is forced to confront French state collusion in the Holocaust and to reflect upon his own divided loyalties as practising Jew and police inspector: 'Sam Benamou, juif de stricte observance et, néanmoins, fonctionnnaire de police?'[39] Yet, in this novel, the empathic listener has been deceived, tricked into an identification and investment in the past of Sylberstein that is pure illusion. As he travels between France and East Berlin, this sense of disorientation and betrayal is made visible in stories of war crimes and the foundation myths of East German society.

Unlike the other novels of this chapter, *Pas de kaddish pour Sylberstein* makes no extended reference to the concentration camps and investigates instead the survivor stories of perpetrators, German and Ukrainian. The answers to Sylberstein/Kravéniouk's past lie in the activities of the SS Kommando Jung Siegfried and its operations in Ukraine and Byelorussia. The brutality of the killings and Kravéniouk's reign of terror are the backdrop for the switching of identities which see Kravéniouk reinvent himself with the identity papers of the Jew Simon Sylberstein whom he believes to have perished. The utter chaos of the final months of the war is emphasised, as well as the ways in which former Nazi officers were able to reconstitute new lives for themselves, in this case in East Germany, having been re-educated to be faithful Communist Party members. The novel makes much of the role of Moscow in this process and the collusion of the American secret services. But, as the novel progresses, it is evident that such rehabilitation has not prevented continuing loyalties to National Socialism, both amongst the wartime and successor generations in Germany. Celebrations in honour of a Nazi local hero, Horst Wessel, in East Berlin in the novelistic present, although presented parodically, reinforce this. In addition, the novel makes clear how the East German authorities continued to profit from the actions of their Nazi predecessors, selling pillaged Jewish art work on markets abroad as a means of generating further income. With the ending of the Cold War, this tangled web of perpetrators and victims brings to light troubling wartime legacies that include expedient political reinventions, identity theft and a trade in stolen art works.[40] *Pas de kaddish pour Sylberstein* suggests that our moral certitudes about the war – its victors and victims – are becoming less rather than more secure with the passing of time.

In its representation of collective guilt and responsibility, *Pas de kaddish pour Sylberstein* builds on the opening up of archives and revised war narratives attendant on the collapse of communism post-1989. As in *Les Orpailleurs* and *KZ*, international circuits of memory are symbolised by the movements of the main protagonist as Benamou moves from Paris to East Berlin and back in order to reconstruct the past of Sylberstein/ Kravéniouk and Stoltz. In terms of German war narratives, commonly held images and stereotypes are reworked. The national mythology of the German Democratic Republic as the inheritor of the anti-fascist struggle is dismantled in the novel with the revelation of the rehabilitation of selected SS officers to serve the ruling communist elites. While the relationship between Germany and a wider Jewish diaspora is revisited when Benamou's Jewish colleagues refuse the Manichaean depictions of victim and perpetrator, commenting on the cultural intersections that bind the Jewish community and Germany, above all in the realm of music: 'Entre nous et les Allemands, c'est une histoire d'amour',[41] the novel is at its most challenging in its portrayal of the impact of 'delayed memories' of the war years on the successor generation. Judith Stoltz, daughter of Rudi, a father whom she believed to be a founding member of the GDR political class, crumbles as his past as a former Nazi is uncovered. Benamou himself is reluctant to believe that the man in whose name he has investigated is in fact a Ukrainian war criminal who has prospered within the very community he attempted to eradicate. Throughout the novel, responsibility for the confused national and international narratives of war is laid at the feet of an older generation who has not responded adequately to the social demand for war memories of their children and grandchildren.

However, the novel ends on a moment of miraculous survival. As Benamou and other practising Jews in his local synagogue meet to recite the kaddish for the spirit of Sylberstein, wherever and whenever he may have perished, an ageing American enters the room. Having read an advertisement placed in the New York *Jewish Chronicle* for further information on Simon Sylberstein, he has travelled to Paris to announce that he is the real Simon Sylberstein: 'nous sommes tous morts là-bas. Mais moi, j'ai survécu'.[42] As a literal return of the dead, the Sylberstein of the book's ending offers a message of hope. All is not lost, the past is not irretrievable and the survivor's voice is finally heard. From the Ukraine to America and Paris, Sylberstein's story is one of resurrection and recognition in the company of fellow Jews and a celebration of endurance. Yet the novel's positive conclusion also underscores the many odd and uncomfortable couplings that have structured the whole narrative. The real Simon Sylberstein, like his fake Parisian counterpart, is also an antiques dealer in an image of the intersecting destinies of two men, poles apart, yet whom Benamou's investigation has brought together.

Pas de kaddish pour Sylberstein ultimately challenges compartmentalised narratives of the Second World War. In this fiction, perpetrators have taken on the mantle of victims and national war fictions of fortitude and heroism are effectively debunked. Via the central figure of Benamou, the representative of the successor generation, the novel makes evident the confusion and disorientation such revisionist histories bring. Post-war certitudes are undermined, such as the moral probity of elders, and the testimonial process is flawed and corrupted by the perpetrator who exploits the compassion and tolerance of his listener. While 'Simon Sylberstein' may return, his several post-war lives demonstrate the fragmented war legacies one generation has bequeathed another.

Conclusion

The crime novels discussed in this chapter have made visible the contribution of popular culture to debates on the legacies of war in 1980s and 1990s France in three significant respects. Firstly, they point to the development of hybrid forms of literary fictions, novels which combine historical investigation and imaginative reconstruction. In these decades, a new generation of crime writers emerged who brought different questions and concerns to the depiction of events lived through by their parents and grandparents. The sense of the passage of time appears to have reinvigorated debates on what and how to remember the past and highlighted the urgency of constructing a historically accurate depiction of the past for readers who may have no direct experience of the war years. Literary narratives, in this context, have offered the possibility to bridge the gap between historical knowledge and private memory. This historicising impulse may well explain the common recourse to the testimony of the survivor, an account which validates the primacy of lived experience but also requires contextualisation and interpretation. All the novels analysed in this chapter make use of the survivor's story as a point of access into wider histories, both that of the victim and the perpetrator. Yet, they also show up the pitfalls of overreliance on received narratives of persecution and extermination for an understanding of the past, whether this is the guilt and betrayal expressed by the survivor-witness in *KZ retour vers l'enfer,* the camp complicities of Isy Szalcman in *Les Orpailleurs* or the false testimony of Kravéniouk/Sylberstein in *Pas de kaddish pour Sylberstein.* In all cases, the novels examined here highlight the need to interrogate what appear to be polarised moral, national or ethnic oppositions.

Secondly, these crime fictions exemplify the shift in focus from war fictions located within the closed circuit of familial memory to their dissemination via open circuits of public memory. While the crime fictions of the 1950s and 1960s, examined in Chapter 2, charted the eruption of family secrets into the narrative present, crime fictions of the 1980s and 1990s are more likely to address memory made visible in the public arenas of the media and the justice system. Such novels are less preoccupied with family shame and more with the national and transnational ramifications of war memories and their significance for contemporary society. The role of successor generations in enabling testimony and survivor stories to emerge is central to these texts, as is the moral burden of accommodating often disquieting war memories. The 'vicissitudes of listening', in the words of Dori Laub, are emphasised in all three novels as successor generation interlocutors adopt listening defences in order to cope with the intensity of the traumatic memories encountered. This draws a sense of outrage and despair in *KZ;* respect and understanding in *Les Orpailleurs,* and withdrawal and confusion in *Pas de kaddish pour Sylberstein.* In these novels, listening to survivor stories is not a neutral activity and has personal implications for the listener. It requires rethinking conventional understandings of the war years and brings new anxieties and concerns to bear on why, how and what to remember as the generation that comes after.

Finally, all the crime fictions in this chapter address troubling questions of national and transnational guilt and responsibility. The novels discussed here invoke, to varying degrees, French complicity in the deportation of Jews, whether this be at the level of familial complicity, as in *Les Orpailleurs,* or in terms of the Vichy regime itself, its police force and its functionaries, as in *Pas de kaddish pour Sylberstein.* Equally striking is the use of the figure of the onlooker, the complicit witness, incarnated in *KZ* and *Les Orpailleurs* in the person of the Polish villagers who profit from the emplacement of extermination camps in their region. The reverberations of such complicity are evident in both novels' depiction of such *lieux de mémoire* in the textual present and the challenges they pose for what is remembered and what omitted from public discourses on the war years. Ultimately, all three novels underscore how unresolved conflicts from the war years continue to afflict national communities today and implicate peoples and cultures beyond Nazi Germany in the perpetration of the Holocaust.

It is these European circuits of memory that emerge as a powerful public discourse on war in these novels. As the trials for crimes against humanity in France reaffirmed, the courtroom was not always the most propitious place for interrogating the past. The project of judging events that took place more than forty or fifty years earlier was one fraught with difficulties and could not hope to stand in for a collective reckoning with the past. Yet, even in the light of what many believed to be the failings of such a legalistic process, the urgency of engaging critically with the past was never in doubt, notably via the memories and fictions of survivors which spoke to and across generations. For as Luisa Passerini asserts: 'The real challenge is not to ignore the horrors of the past, but to deepen our knowledge of the worst aspects of European history. In pursuit of this kind of knowledge we need at the same time to know how to find elements of humanity and positive intersubjectivity.'[43] It is the value of these intersubjective and intergenerational encounters that is reaffirmed in such crime fictions.

Notes

1   Luisa Passerini, 'Memories of resistance, resistances of memory', in Helmut Peitsch, Charles Burdett and Claire Gorrara (eds), *European Memories of the Second World War* (Oxford: Berghahn Books, 1999), pp. 288–96 (p. 289).

2   See 'The politics of war memory and commemoration: contexts, structures and dynamics', in T. G. Ashplant, Graham Dawson and Michael Roper (eds), *The Politics of War Memory and Commemoration* (London: Routledge, 2000), pp. 3–85, for discussion of the modalities of memory in these decades.

3   Annette Wieviorka, 'From survivor to witness: voices from the Shoah', Jay Winter and Emmanuel Sivan (eds), *War and Remembrance in the Twentieth Century* (Cambridge: Cambridge University Press, 1999), pp. 125–41 (p. 133).

4   Wieviorka, 'From survivor to witness', p. 137. As Wieviorka notes in this chapter, the trial of Adolf Eichmann in Jerusalem in 1960 was a watershed moment, marking the emergence of the Holocaust in France, the USA and Israel as a fundamental part of Jewish identity which demanded public recognition.

5   Passerini, 'Memories of resistance, resistances of memory', p. 289.
6   See Annette Wieviorka, '60 ans après Auschwitz: histoire et mémoire', *L'Esprit Créateur*, 65:3 (2005), 40–8, for an overview of the shifting configurations of Holocaust memory within a French cultural frame.
7   See Joan B. Wolf, *Harnessing the Holocaust: The Politics of Memory in France* (Palo Alto, CA: Stanford University Press, 2004) for an analysis of the constructions of the Holocaust in French public discourse in the post-war decades.
8   For a discussion of Holocaust denial in France in these decades, above all the controversy surrounding the publication of Roger Garaudy's *Les Mythes fondateurs de la politique isralienne* (1995), see Chapter 7, 'Denying the Holocaust in France: the past and present of an illusion', in Richard Golsan, *Vichy's Afterlife: History and Counterhistory in Postwar France* (Lincoln, NE: University of Nebraska Press, 2000).
9   Wolf, *Harnessing the Holocaust*, p. 198.
10   See Wolf, Chapter 6, '"Why the war haunts us": Vichy on trial', *Harnessing the Holocaust*, pp. 128–58.
11   For discussion of the campaign for recognition of the *rafle du Vélodrome d'Hiver* as state-sponsored persecution, see Wieviorka, '60 ans après Auschwitz: histoire et mémoire', 45–6, and Wolf, Chapter 7, 'Mitterrand, Papon and the politics of historical responsibility', *Harnessing the Holocaust*, pp. 159–88 (pp. 160–6).
12   See Nancy Wood, 'Memory on trial in contemporary France', *Vectors of Memory: Legacies of Trauma in Postwar Europe* (Oxford: Berg, 1999), pp. 113–42, for a discussion of the courtroom context and the legal and historical debates surrounding the definition of crimes against humanity in France in these decades.
13   Cited in Wood, 'Memory on trial in contemporary France', p. 117.
14   Jean Leguay: representative of the Vichy police in the occupied zone, 1 May 1942 to the end of 1943; indicted for crimes against humanity in 1979; died in 1989 just as his case was being put forward for prosecution. René Bousquet: Vichy head of police, 18 April 1942 to December 1943; indicted for crimes against humanity in 1991; assassinated in June 1993, three days before his trial. Maurice Papon: secretary-general of Vichy's regional administration in the Bordeaux region, the Gironde Prefecture, 1 June 1942 to 22 August 1994; tried for crimes against humanity in 1997–98; sentenced to 10 years in prison for complicity in crimes against humanity. Paul Touvier: head of the intelligence section of the militia in the Savoy region, April 1943 to September 1944; tried for crimes against humanity in 1994, sentenced to life imprisonment.
15   For a critical assessment of the courtroom context and the role of the historian as expert witness, see Henry Rousso, *La Hantise du passé (entretien avec Philippe Petit)* (Paris: Les Editions Textuels, 1998).

16 Wood, 'Memory on trial in contemporary France', p. 124.

17 Wood, 'Memory on trial in contemporary France', p. 132.

18 Simone Lagrange, a child survivor of the Holocaust, appeared in edited footage of the Barbie trial broadcast on French television. She also proved to be a moving interviewee in Marcel Ophuls' Oscar award-winning documentary film, *Hotel Terminus: The Life and Times of Klaus Barbie* (1988).

19 See, for example, Alain Wagneur, *Homicide à bon marché* (Paris: Gallimard, 1996) in which the death of a father coincides with his detective son's investigation into the identity of a mutilated body. The connection between the two is the father's past as a prisoner of war; Joseph Bialot, *La Nuit du souvenir* (Paris: Gallimard, 1990) in which the kidnapping of the main protagonist's grandchild leads back to memories of his deportation; Claude Amoz, *L'Ancien Crime* (Paris: Payot et Rivages, 1999), in which the wartime betrayal of a resister is belatedly discovered to emanate from within his family; Gérard Delteil, *Mort d'un satrape rouge* (Paris: Métailié, 1995), the story of a despotic local mayor and resistance hero murdered in the narrative present and the investigation of a local journalist; Claude Klotz, *Kobar* (Paris: Albin Michel, 1992) in which the titular character discovers his father's death at Maidenek in 1943 and pursues the man who denounced him; Hélène Couturier, *Sarah* (Paris: Rivages, 1997) in which a niece goes in search of her deceased aunt's past and discovers a repressed story of wartime persecution as Jews; Ramon Mercader (Thierry Jonquet), *Du passé faisons table rase* (Paris: Albin Michel, 1982), an exposé of the wartime past of a fictionalised leader of the French Communist Party and how the party has maintained his secret by stealth and murder.

20 The three writers in this chapter were born during or after the war years: Delteil (1939), Jonquet (1954) and Konop (1948).

21 The following editions of the novels have been published: Gérard Delteil, *KZ retour vers l'enfer*: Paris: Carrère, 1987; Paris: Editions Métailié, 1998. Thierry Jonquet, *Les Orpailleurs*: Editions Gallimard, 1993, 1998, 2010; Paris: France Loisirs, 1998 and Paris: Editions France Loisirs-Le Cercle polar, 2003. Konop, *Pas de kaddish pour Sylberstein*: Paris: Editions Gallimard, 1993; Paris: Le Grand Livre du mois, 1997. References will be to the following editions: Delteil: Editions Métailié, 1998, Jonquet: Editions Gallimard, 1993, and Konop: Editions Gallimard, 1993.

22 Dori Laub, 'Bearing witness, or the vicissitudes of listening', in Shoshana Felman and Dori Laub, *Testimony: Crises of Witnessing in Literature, Psychoanalysis and History* (London: Routledge, 1992), pp. 57–74 (p. 74).

23 These terms are taken from: Chapter 4, 'History, memory and moral judgement after the Holocaust: Marcel Ophuls' *Hotel Terminus: The Life and Times of Klaus Barbie*', in Susan Suleiman, *Crises of Memory and the Second World War* (Cambridge, MA: Harvard University Press, 2006), pp. 77–105 (pp. 77–8).

24 On his website, Delteil acknowledges that the inspiration for this fictional concentration camp is Buchenwald: http://delteil.voila.net/page3/index.html (accessed 20 April 2011).

25 Laub, 'Bearing witness, or the vicissitudes of listening', p. 57.

26 Delteil makes reference to Rousset's *Les Jours de notre mort* (1947) but he could equally have cited Rousset's *L'Univers concentrationnaire*, published in the first wave of chronicle-testimonies in 1946.

27 The psychological strategies required to act as perpetrator or to survive horror are discussed by Tzvetan Todorov in *Facing the Extreme: Moral Life in the Concentration Camps* (New York: Henry Holt, 1997).

28 Delteil, *KZ*, p. 283 (things revealed themselves to be so complex, so unlike all sorts of commonly accepted models …).

29 Delteil, *KZ*, p. 258 (they have got that smell of Jews, and that one really looks like one).

30 Delteil, *KZ*, pp. 269–70 (the splendid motorway which we were travelling along together had been built by a workforce taken from the concentration camps – the transportation of enormous blocks of base materials had cost the lives of thousands of shaven-headed slaves).

31 For related readings of this novel, see Claire Gorrara, 'Reflections on crime and punishment: memories of the Holocaust in recent French crime fiction', *Yale French Studies*, 108 (2005), 131–45.

32 Jonquet, *Les Orpailleurs*, p. 147 ('Yes, that's it, everything went on as if he had never left the camp. There was this life which went by, day after day amongst us, a pretend life really, while the other, the real one, carried on "over there"').

33 See Tzvetan Todorov, *Les Abus de la mémoire* (Paris: Arléa, 1995) for the formulation of two uses of memory, literal and exemplary, and their relationship to contemporary memory culture.

34 Jonquet, *Les Orpailleurs*, p. 311 (She [Lintz] remembered the Auschwitz museum, so well maintained and so jealously guarded. Birkenau was more like a waste land, a rubbish heap of memory).

35 Canada was the term used for the barracks where the possessions of new arrivals to the camp were sorted. The most valuable items were dispatched to Germany. However, working in Canada gave deportees various opportunities for trafficking useful items.

36 Jonquet, *Les Orpailleurs*, p. 307.

37 Jonquet, *Les Orpailleurs*, p. 308 (You are in the middle of the largest cemetery in the world. There is not one clod of earth, not one, which does not have mixed within it human ashes. Millions and millions of bodies … burned, and buried under this tender grass. The crematoria flames could be seen for more than twenty kilometres around).

38 The narrative conceit of false testimony had captured French public opinion in the early 1990s due to the controversy surrounding Benjamin

Wilkomirski's novel *Fragments*, first published in Switzerland in 1995. In this text, the author claimed to have 'recovered' his past as a child Holocaust survivor following therapy. This proved to be a complete invention.

39 Konop, *Pas de kaddish pour Sylberstein*, p. 19 (Sam Benamou, a strictly observant Jew and yet a police functionary?).

40 The 1990s and 2000s saw the publication of a wave of French crime novels built around wartime Jewish dispossession. These include: Georges-Jean Arnaud, *Spoliation* (Paris: Fleuve noir, 2000), Stéphane Geffray, *Les Teutons flingueurs* (Paris: Editions Baleine,1999), Jack Chaboud, *Le Tronc de la veuve* (Paris: Le Passage, 2003), Hannelore Cayre, *Toiles de maître* (Paris: Editions Métailié, 2005), Franck Pavloff, *Le Vent des fous* (Paris: Gallimard, 1993), Noël Simsolo, *Wazemmes* (Marseille: L'Ecailler du Sud, 2005).

41 Konop, *Pas de kaddish pour Sylberstein*, p. 110 (Between us and the Germans, it's a love story).

42 Konop, *Pas de kaddish pour Sylberstein*, p. 150 (We all died there. But I survived).

43 Passerini, 'Memories of resistance, resistances of memory', p. 296.

5

Mobilising memory: reading the Second World War in children's crime fiction of the 1990s and 2000s

The 1990s and 2000s in France saw a number of memorial taboos surrounding the Second World War publicly overturned. The most symbolic of these acts occurred during the speech delivered by newly elected President Jacques Chirac on 16 July 1995 to mark the fifty-third anniversary of the *rafle du Vélodrome d'Hiver*. For the first time in national history, a French head of state officially acknowledged the active support of the Vichy regime and its agents in the persecution and extermination of Jews resident in France. The language of the speech underscored a collective sense of shame at state-sponsored complicity in such events and the damage it had inflicted on cherished French ideals: 'La France, patrie des Lumières et des Droits de l'Homme, terre d'accueil et d'asile, la France, ce-jour-là, accomplissait l'irréparable'.[1]

This chapter will discuss representations of wartime Jewish persecution in children's crime fiction of the 1990s and 2000s and their mobilisation as part of a civic memory of the recent past intended to inform and inspire younger generations. It will begin by examining the context of the 1990s and 2000s in France and a reframing of memory which allowed a more plural set of war memories to gain public prominence. It will then proceed to examine two key cultural arenas for the transmission of war narratives for younger generations: the classroom and children's fiction. In analysing the cultural mediation of the war years in these two contexts, this chapter will map out a civic memory of the Second World War structured around questions of collective responsibility and an ethics of remembrance. It will then examine representations of the Second World War in three crime novels aimed at younger readers and how these fictions engage with such a reframing of the war years. These novels are: Robert Boudet's *Mon prof est un espion* (1991), Mireille Szac's *Un lourd silence* (1999) and Romain Slocombe's *Qui se souvient de Paula?* (2008).

Ultimately, this chapter will argue that crime fiction for younger readers furthers understanding of the complex negotiations required to transmit war stories to generations for whom the past is another country.

Reframing the past

During the 1990s and 2000s, France, embodied above all in its state institutions, came to engage constructively with a more diverse range of wartime memories than in previous decades. Jacques Chirac's unambiguous condemnation of the Vichy regime set the tone for greater recognition of France's national responsibility for communities that had suffered under wartime occupation or been active in support of France's liberation. This recognition had practical consequences including improved pensions rights for colonial troops who had fought on behalf of the Allies; belated compensation for people whose parents had been deported from France as a result of anti-Semitic persecution, and the commissioning of the Mattéoli report in 1997 which investigated the pillaging of Jewish property under the occupation and the extent to which restitution had been made.[2] It would seem that the time had come for a freeing up of war memories in the public arena, a development that some historians attributed to a changing of the guard at the highest political level.[3] However, as Olivier Wieviorka notes, the competing claims for recognition as a result of wartime suffering also posed great difficulty for state institutions intent on arriving at a coherent and ideally consensual narrative of the wartime past. Rather than nurturing solidarity, such state recognition of past wrongs reinforced what Wieviorka terms 'la balkanisation mémorielle',[4] as the landscape of war memories fractured into mutually hostile territories marked by rival claims for public attention. In addition, the legacy of more recent conflicts, such as the Algerian War, came to accentuate already existent social, political and cultural divisions as groups campaigning for greater consideration of their experiences of immigration, exile and discrimination expressed rancour at the apparent primacy accorded Jewish survivors of wartime deportation. Therefore, while the 1990s and 2000s were a period of productive national exposure to France's wartime past, they were not necessarily indicative of an effective process of coming to terms with the past or the successful transmission of war histories to younger generations of French citizens.

Questions of generational transmission did, however, preoccupy state educators and legislators, as well as filmmakers and writers in these decades.[5] These were years when it was considered imperative to disseminate further knowledge and understanding of the war years and to communicate a sense of collective responsibility. The political capital to be gained – and indeed forfeited – in attempting to mobilise such powerful discourses in the classroom was well illustrated when, on 16 May 2007, newly elected French President, Nicolas Sarkozy instructed secondary school teachers to read out in class the last letter of seventeen-year-old communist resister Guy Môquet to his parents. Môquet was executed by firing squad for acts of resistance on 22 October 1941. Sarkozy intended this gesture to symbolise his commitment to the Resistance as a model of national duty and self-sacrifice. However, this initiative drew negative reactions from the teaching establishment and was interpreted as a cynical political ploy that had little respect for the historical specificities of the period, creating an overly sentimentalised image of the young man as a martyr and misrepresenting his ideological affiliations. Yet, as author Alexandre Jardin was to write in his polemical exposé of his own family's wartime heritage, the next generation had a responsibility towards the past and were key *passeurs de mémoire*: 'si nous ne sommes pas coupables des actes de nos pères et grands-pères … nous restons responsables de notre regard'.[6] It was the filtering of this perspective on the past which gained in importance as the generations who had lived through events began to disappear. Children and adolescents of the 1990s and 2000s would not necessarily have direct family experience of the occupation and were likely to rely on the school curriculum and popular culture, above all via the internet, for their understanding of such a past. Such a shift in the cultural mediation of the past posed challenges for the school system: what should such children learn of French wartime experiences? Which events should be the focus of history teaching and which explanatory frames should be applied to the documents and material presented? How could fiction and film complement such teachings and how could such narratives be made relevant to contemporary debates and conflicts? Indeed, how could the legacies of the wartime past be mobilised to help shape national identity and culture? In the 1990s and 2000s, it was possible to envisage a less differentiated approach to the Second World War than in previous decades and the integration of such a historical period into an expanded French memorial landscape. The legacies of the Second World War could be discussed alongside other contested wars and conflicts and feature as one element in a civic education intended to form young citizens for the future. By focusing on the lessons the war years might yield, historians noted that memories of the Second World War could be used to encourage an ethics of responsibility in younger generations, as well as greater sensitivity towards the personal and social costs of discrimination, persecution and exclusion.[7]

Transmitting civic memories of war

One of the key cultural arenas for transmission of a civic memory of the past is the classroom. The teaching of history, above all, can be organised to bring distant events back to life and to give the past a value and significance that can affect the way students think, believe and act in the present. In his polemical essay on memory, community and the republican idea in contemporary France, Jean-Philippe Mathy tackles the 'transmission problems' of Republican history in contemporary France. He focuses upon Editions du Seuil's didactic guides to French history aimed at children and identifies them as symptomatic of France's 'uneasy relationship to the national past and the European future'.[8] Reading a selection of these pocket guides, Mathy notes anxiety about what should (but has not been) communicated to younger generations via the public school system and he interprets the guides as indicative of 'a lack of collective memory, a fateful break in the temporal chain of cultural transmission'.[9] In the case of the French Resistance, Mathy's concerns regarding transmission problems have some validity. Lucie Aubrac's contribution to the series on this subject projects an image of unalloyed heroism.[10] In *La Résistance expliquée à mes petits-enfants*, Aubrac focuses on the bravery of individuals, both well-known and now forgotten, and gives a largely Gaullist reading of events, promoting the actions of the Free French Forces and the military contribution of the French Resistance to territorial liberation. Aubrac's account for children fails to address the political and ideological differences that divided resisters and her vision of unequivocal resistance unity can be accused of avoiding the harsh realities of a more complex war history. Yet, while we might interpret Aubrac's defence of the Resistance as evidence of the cultural damage wrought to such a wartime memory in the 1990s, the interpretative frame within which the resistance legacy is positioned is revealing. Aubrac's text makes repeated reference to the human rights abuse suffered by marginalised groupings, such as the Jews, and ends with an imaginary child interlocutor stating: 'vous vous [resisters] êtes battus et vous avez gagné sur la haine, le racisme et la violence. S'il le fallait, nous serions prêts à faire comme vous!'[11] This discourse of human rights and collective responsibility is equally present in classroom representations of the Second World War during the 1990s and 2000s, particularly the depiction of the war as a global conflict with ramifications beyond France's national borders.

During the 1950s and 1960s, the Second World War in French history textbooks was presented in a highly condensed and selective form. This is well illustrated by Editions Hachette's 1964 history of France where the Second World War in France is represented visually by a photograph of triumphant liberation and no mention is made of Pétain, the Vichy regime, collaboration or anti-Semitic persecution.[12] By the mid-1980s, the Holocaust had begun to be taught on French history programmes and the pedagogy of the Second World War has developed in sophistication and changed in focus. By 2010, the Second World War was being taught at all levels in primary and secondary school, with 30 to 50 per cent of such teaching devoted to the Holocaust. The structuring and organisation of such teaching is indicative of the educative aims of the history programme of the 2000s. At levels CM1 or CM2 (children between the ages of nine and eleven), the Second World War is identified as a war of annihilation, with transnational dimensions, and the programme instructs teachers to focus specifically on the extermination of the Jews and the Gypsies, categorising the Holocaust as a crime against humanity.[13] At secondary school level, such an approach continues under the thematic 'world wars and hopes for peace' where students are asked to consider war over the twentieth century and to read across conflicts, identifying the shifting nature of the prosecution of war over the century. Indeed, by 2010, it was possible to require students to engage in a meta-historical reflection on the evolution of memories of the Second World War since 1945 with the inclusion of one such question on a Baccalauréat Général written examination paper for history. This subject asked students to discuss a range of historical documents: a wartime poster, a commemorative stamp, extracts from history textbooks from different decades and Jacques Chirac's 16 July 1995 speech on the fifty-third anniversary of the *rafle du Vélodrome d'Hiver*.[14] Here, for the first time, not only the war years but the multiple and shifting memorial discourses to which they had given rise were the subject of analysis. In broadly pedagogical terms, such material would indicate that, over the 1990s and 2000s, the Second World War has been internationalised (both in territorial and ideological terms); placed in an expanded chronological frame (wars of the twentieth century); harnessed to a human rights discourse (shaped by the aftermath of the Holocaust); and inflected by debates on the legacies of war for present-day society.

If the classroom can be viewed as a key cultural arena for the transmission of civic memories of war, contemporary war fiction for younger readers promotes similar messages. These accentuate the story of the individual and raise awareness of the reader's ethical responsibility towards the past. In her essay on 'storying war', Mitzi Myers points to the didactic function of much fiction for children set during wartime.[15] However, she debunks the common perception that such fiction is overwhelmingly escapist, unsophisticated or nationalistic, commenting that such fiction for children may 'inculcate patriotic moral values or, more often, question the morality of war'.[16] For Myers, current children's war stories are written in a different context to earlier fictions, with contemporary authors better equipped than their predecessors to engage with the moral and social realities of past and present genocides, the Holocaust, ethnic cleansing and fears of nuclear disaster or global catastrophe. In recent years, this has led to children's stories being published that give accessible social and cultural histories of war, tackling issues of exile and displacement, escape and survival, and contesting national and cultural stereotypes.[17] Indeed, Myers asserts that these fictions often adopt an ethical stance promoting the values of 'humane living' at a time of social, political and ideological violence.[18] In their depiction of the realities of war, such texts prove themselves more open than other fictional genres for younger readers to cross-writing, traversing the boundaries between fiction and history and children's fiction and adult fiction.

More than any other conflict in recent years, the Second World War fits this expanded frame for children's war stories. As studies of children's war fiction attest, contemporary writers of children's fiction about the Second World War struggle with contradictory impulses, indicative of the pivotal role fiction plays in shaping children's understanding of the past. How can such authors provide a historically accurate representation of events but maintain dramatic tension and interest? How should they balance the need for truth-telling against the need for reassurance and 'sparing the child'?[19] How might they craft a fiction which acknowledges the limited historical understanding of the child or younger reader but assumes its moral obligation to communicate often unspeakable acts to younger readers? In France of the 1990s and 2000s, examples of Second World War cross-writing aimed at younger readers engage with these issues. Michel Quint's *Effroyables Jardins* charges its teenage readers with deconstructing cultural stereotypes of the German soldier via the intergenerational motif of the clown and the tragedy of war.[20] In Philippe Grimbert's bestseller, *Un secret,* the narrator's quest to discover more of his family's wartime past leads to the discovery of his Jewish origins and the existence of a lost half-brother, deported to Auschwitz aged eight, who haunts the narrator's imaginary as a ghostly presence.[21] In these and other war fictions of the 1990s and 2000s published in France, such as Tatiana de Rosnay's *Elle s'appelait Sarah*,[22] child and adult protagonists grapple with national and familial legacies and their responsibility to know and understand more about wartime events in France, above all the Holocaust. This chapter will now examine the reading frame of French children's crime fiction, before exploring representations of the Second World War in Robert Boudet's *Mon prof est un espion* (1991), Mireille Szac's *Un lourd silence* (1999) and Romain Slocombe's *Qui se souvient de Paula?* (2008) and the mobilisation of war memories for an ethics of responsibility.

Storying war in children's crime fiction: an ethics of responsibility

In the early and mid-twentieth century, detective and crime fiction for children was largely underdeveloped in France, limited to translations of American and English classics for adolescent readers, such as the Sherlock Holmes stories of Arthur Conan Doyle, and with only a limited range of French or francophone adventure stories available.[23] Such a situation can be attributed to prevailing views amongst the cultural establishment that such popular fiction had the potential to corrupt the minds of young readers with tales of transgression and misdemeanour. It was, like other genres of children's fiction, 'une littérature placée sous surveillance'.[24] By the 1950s and 1960s, with the success of foreign serial mysteries, such as those of Enid Blyton and Caroline Keene, the market for children's detective and crime fiction expanded, although it remained a genre associated with conservative social and aesthetic values. In 1986, with the launch of Editions Syros' Souris noire collection, aimed at seven to ten year-old readers, the landscape of children's crime fiction in France changed beyond recognition. The Souris noire collection positioned itself as the children's equivalent of the *roman noir*, promising thrilling fiction which would tackle some of the darkest secrets of contemporary society and keep young readers on the edge of their seats until the final page.[25] Celebrated authors of adult crime fiction published in the series, such as Didier Daeninckx, Patrick Mosconi, Daniel Pennac and Jean-Hugues Oppel, and much was made of the series' intention to break the taboos of children's fiction. By opening the way for such crosswriting between adult and children's fiction, the series encouraged other publishers to imitate its success and pay greater attention to children's crime fiction as a means of engaging with the social issues of the day, both within and beyond the classroom.[26] More than two decades later, specialist crime fictions for children are less visible as part of the marketing strategy of publishing houses. Rather, children's fiction with a crime motif or structure has been integrated into generalist collections as a staple of the French market.

In terms of the Second World War in children's crime fiction, this historical period has attracted a number of accomplished writers, such as Didier Daeninckx, Béatrice Nicodème, Liliane Korb and Laurence Lefèvre, Jean-Paul Nozière and Thierry Crifo.[27] For example, Daeninckx's *Galadio* (2010) approaches the build-up to war and the war years via the perspective of a mixed-race adolescent, Galadio, born of a German mother and French Sudanese father, a *tirailleur sénégalais* stationed in Germany as part of the French occupying forces at the end of the First World War. From this ex-centric perspective, Daeninckx explores not only the rising discrimination and persecution of minority populations in pre-war Germany but also the prosecution of war in the African sub-continent from an African perspective.[28] What has made the crime format such an apposite vehicle for writing war fictions for children is its questing structure whereby, as in *Galadio*, a child or adolescent goes in search of a buried wartime past. In recent decades, this quest in Second World War fiction has been constructed around the discovery of crimes committed against the Jewish population; the 16 July 1942 *rafle du Vélodrome d'Hiver* being emblematic in this respect. It is here that the novels for children probe questions of ethical responsibility. For, in common with adult war fiction of the same period, the quest to unearth the past leads inexorably to lost Jewish children and the culpability and responsibility of the French state and its agents. The ethical charge of such novels lies in how such memories are represented in narrative terms and the extent to which they generate a broader reflection on racism, discrimination and persecution.

Robert Boudet's *Mon prof est un espion* was first published in 1991 in Editions Casterman's Mystères collection, aimed at nine to twelve-year-old readers, and has been republished three times, most recently in 2010 in Casterman's generalist Poche collection.[29] Introducing readers to the child-detective Max le Futé, the volume was well received critically and recommended as one of the 1,001 books for younger readers by the Direction des Ecoles in 1997 as part of its primary school programme.[30] The novel approaches the Second World War via the perspective of Max and his band of friends, Bébé Plume and Sonia, who investigate the mysterious behaviour of a replacement French teacher at their school. Mr

Forestier's black sunglasses and unconventional behaviour mark him out as different to the rest of the teaching body. As Max trails Louis Forestier's movements outside school, he comes to suspect that Mr Forestier is an industrial spy and, using the advice of his friend, retired police inspector Charvin, he attempts to expose Louis Forestier's criminal behaviour. However, as the novel reaches its denouement, discordant elements begin to destabilise such a conventional crime reading of Louis Forestier's unpredictable behaviour. His secret is revealed to have its origins in the Second World War and the identity of his birth parents, a local Jewish family denounced in April 1944 by neighbours and who perished in Buchenwald.[31] As their child David Steinberg, he is hastily adopted by a local family and renamed, only to discover his real identity, many years later, at the bedside of his dying adoptive mother.

In this crime fiction for younger children, the war years are evoked in fragments and only at the end of a false quest for culpability which sees the supposed perpetrator, Louis Forestier, transformed into the victim, David Steinberg. Indeed, the past appears scrambled throughout the text, a conundrum very much in the mode of the playground riddles with which Max entertains the other children. Even with the support of an adult guide, Charvin, Max misinterprets clues and fails to see the bigger picture. Yet, the narrative infers, all the elements are in place to understand what appears to be the mysterious identity of Louis Forestier for the children and which a rereading would reveal. For example, the fictionalised setting of the narrative is the town of Darcy, etymologically reminiscent of Drancy; the Jewish quarter where Louis/David was born is demolished at the end of the war to make way for the local refuse site, a comment on the evacuation of Jewish memory from the local community; and, on the first encounter with the mix of dates and letters which Louis/David uses to locate his wartime origins, Charvin notes, in bemusement: 'pour l'instant, c'est de l'hébreu', inadvertently identifying the racial marker at the centre of the mystery.[32]

The pieces of the jigsaw puzzle finally come together when the child-detectives are faced with documentary evidence from the war period. These are photographs of Louis/David's parents, newspaper cuttings announcing their death, and then, finally, the testimony of Louis/David, the child survivor, a character unaware of his Jewish origins until well into adulthood. Indeed, 'David Steinberg' is the privileged embodiment of the past in this novel for younger children. For this is not a tale of death and destruction but miraculous survival: a saved Jewish child. However, this story of redemption via the charitable actions of his neighbours is tinged with a sense of quiet melancholia and a pervasive anxiety about where Louis/David fits in and who he might be. By the end of the narrative he elects to return to the USA, a displaced person in France and forever other to the culture in which he was born.

The effect of such revelations on the child protagonists is more muted than in the other novels in this chapter and the narrative could be considered to have significantly softened the war story for children. This may be due to the targeted age range, nine to twelve-year-olds, the youngest category of readers for children's crime fiction, and its 'reader-protective strategies' which offer, 'protective censoring and intentional limiting of the reader's understanding … '.[33] These reader-protective strategies can be traced in three narrative developments. Firstly, while Max and his companions uncover secret histories from the war years, the deportation and extermination of the Jews are largely eclipsed. The deaths of Louis/David's parents are elliptically noted as 'la fin abominable' in a short newspaper report.[34] Secondly, this submerged history of French wartime persecution of the Jewish population does not jeopardise the status of respected authority figures in the text, above all those related to the police. Charvin, the retired police inspector, reveals that he joined the *maquis* after having refused to take part in *la rafle de la rue des Moulins* as a young recruit. No culpability can be attributed to this one representative of the forces of law and order. Thirdly, there is heroic identification with the victim figure, Louis/David, rather than any detailed investigation of the character who denounces the Jewish family to the authorities and who attempts to kill Louis/David years later when the latter threatens to uncover his shameful past. Never named, the nebulous perpetrator is a leading figure in a large electronics company and conforms very much to the narrative schema of the immoral capitalist pitted against the principled child-detective.

Yet the novel does not endorse an overly didactic ending and the moral of the novel is not one of just deserts or justice served but rather the importance of taking responsibility for the past: "'C'est important de savoir qui on est …" dit-elle [Natalie]. Louis Forestier soupire. 'Et quand on découvre qu'on n'est pas qui l'on croyait être.'"[35] Questions of knowledge and understanding are central to the narrative and Louis/David's refusal to pursue his family's persecutor, leaving him instead to live with his conscience, offers a highly individualised response to the legacies of war and one's ethical responsibility to remember. Indeed, while the novel keeps the child protagonists at a safe distance from the horrors of war, in one episode a ghostly connection is made with the present. After Sonia and Max break into Louis/David's house to collect clues for their investigation, Sonia reveals her Jewish identity to Max and the fact that her grandfather died in Buchenwald. When the police rush into the house to arrest the burglars, Sonia faints in shock and wakes to the sight of a group of policemen surrounding her. One might read this episode as creating a deliberate parallelism with the fate of other Jewish children during wartime for whom such a night-time encounter might well have signalled imminent death. In this manifestation alone, *Mon prof est un espion* makes visible the complex filiations between past and present and belies that notion that children can be protected from knowledge of the wartime past.

In Mureille Szac's *Un lourd silence*, first published in 1999, the preface makes explicit the connections between past and present and an authorial intention to expose the child/adolescent reader to the realities of the war and its repercussions. Entitled 'Why I wrote this novel', the author asserts: 'J'ai écris ce livre parce que je suis convaincue d'une chose: chacun d'entre nous a besoin de savoir d'où il vient. Pas de liberté ni d'avenir sans mémoire de son passé, sans l'histoire de ses racines. Nous ne sommes ni coupables ni comptables de ce que firent ceux qui nous ont précédés, mais nous devons savoir.'[36] Here the text alerts the young reader to questions of history and identity and her or his responsibility to assume knowledge of the past, not with the intention of judging others but in order to live with (and not against) the past. Republished in 2009, *Un lourd silence* is aimed at readers of thirteen years and older and is able, as a consequence, to give a more historically detailed and ethically charged narrative of the past than Boudet's *Mon prof est un espion*.[37]

Set in present-day Lyon, *Un lourd silence* affirms the complex interaction of three competing wartime memories: those of collaboration, resistance and Jewish persecution. The adolescent protagonist and first-person narrator, Vincent, aged seventeen, begins the narrative intent on learning more about the identity of his maternal grandfather, Anatole Morel, who died in September 1944 and whose life and death is shrouded in mystery, apart from oblique references to his wartime bravery and sacrifice. Vincent has interpreted this as the resistance epic but, as he discovers more about this shadowy family figure, it is revealed that his grandfather was a member of the Lyon militia and was a close collaborator of Paul Touvier. As he attempts to untangle fiction from fantasy, Vincent develops a friendship with a wartime neighbour of his grandparents, Hanna, a Polish Jew, who was denounced to the authorities by his grandfather and whose daughter, Myrha, died in Auschwitz aged six.

Unlike *Mon prof est un espion*, the Second World War in *Un lourd silence* begins the narrative as a memory which has resonance in the present and is an integral part of present-day family histories. Initially, this memory is cast as a conventional narrative of resistance, albeit a fantasy, as this is the only acceptable form for a family shamed into silence by its collaborationist past. Vincent is deliberately excluded from the family secret and sets out on a mission to reconstruct his grandfather's past that is doomed to failure. The classic tale of resistance is confirmed in the stories his friend Pierre tells of his own father who died in the last days of the war. This was a man who, according to Pierre, 'résistait comme il aurait respiré, sans y penser. Aussi naturel que pour les autres de ne rien faire'.[38] Yet this story of resistance sacrifice and honour gradually fades into the background to be replaced by troubling evocations of collaboration and persecution. Vincent's role, as narrator and protagonist, is to uncover such war narratives and to construct a picture of wartime Lyon which is very different to its present-day reputation as the capital of the Resistance. This focus on an adolescent as an agent of memory forms an important aspect of the narrative. One generation is obliged not only to break the heavy silence of its predecessors but also to interpret their past actions in the light of a value system informed by contemporary affairs and which inevitably reframes the past.

The opposing narratives to the resistance epic – collaboration and Jewish persecution – are personalised in *Un lourd silence* and made real via the fictionalised life histories of Anatole (the persecutor) and Hanna (the victim). Indeed, the narrative suggests at various points that these submerged memories are ever near the surface but blocked out due to the lack of a ready addressee (the next generation) or communal pressures and taboos which make it impossible to confront the past. It is Vincent, the adolescent narrator, who liberates both war stories and whose slow and painful reconstruction of his family's past exemplifies the active memory work required to deliver some form of reconciliation with wartime events. In this sense, although Vincent, like Boudet's Max, has guides and educators from the parental and grandparental generation to help him, such as Pierre, bookshop owner and son of a resister, and his Uncle Jean, his journey of discovery and self-discovery is a lonely one. It causes him to question his own identity and some of the most cherished national war stories, such as that of resistance.

The war story of Jewish persecution in Lyon is recounted three times in the novel and from three different viewpoints as if to reinforce the extent of knowledge about the past but its limited dissemination, above all to younger generations. Firstly, Hanna, the ageing and idiosyncratic Holocaust survivor, sets out in detail her experiences of the slow erosion of citizenship rights for Jews and increasing state surveillance and control. Szac follows other contemporary French novelists in constructing a narrative that condemns French, rather than German, perpetrators. In the extract below, it is the repeated use of the word *français* that condemns the French state, its institutions and agents:

> En juillet 1941, c'est un fonctionnaire français qui a mis un gros tampon rouge 'juive' en travers de ma carte d'identité et qui m'a recensée dans un fichier. Comme une pestiférée. En octobre 1940, c'est la loi française qui nous a imposé un statut à part, à nous les Juifs … Interdit, interdit, tout nous était interdit. Et c'est le gouvernement français qui l'avait décidé. Mes cousins, ceux qui m'avaient fait venir à Lyon, avaient un magasin de chapeaux rue des Pierres-Plantées. Il a été confisqué. Et confié légalement à un bon Français. Et en été 1942, quand des milliers de Juifs ont été raflés à la Guillotière et dans tout Lyon, c'est la police française qui est venue les chercher pour les emmener à l'abattoir.[39]

The telegrammatic style of narration gives a sense of the traumatic events, listing the crimes of the French government in the spiral of despair generated for Jews in occupied France. These events are now part of the French cultural imaginary – Vichy anti-Semitic laws, identity registers, aryanisation – and, as such, this narrative centred on Lyon takes on an emblematic value for the persecution of Jews in France as a whole.

In its second and third iterations, the persecution of Jews in Lyon is given a local colouration as Pierre and his mother provide an account of the round-up of Jews in Lyon on 20 August 1942 to be interned in the camp of Vénissieux. Both narratives provide an account of the Lyon round-ups which add important contextual detail to Hanna's more elliptical narrative. Mme Béroujon, a member of a Christian organisation, reports how the group was able to transport many children from the camp in advance of deportation, taking advantage of the legislative confusion surrounding the status of children in the early stages of the process.[40] Pierre's account provides a more emotive account, saturated in the memory discourses and imagery of state culpability, and which confirms the collaboration of the authorities and the horrific treatment of families and children.[41] The inference is that even when such a story of persecution can be corroborated by eye-witnesses; is transmitted via the family and is locally inflected by virtue of place (Vénissieux), there is still a failure of generational transmission as Vincent remains uncomprehending and shocked by what he learns.

This failure of transmission is amplified in the pendant story to that of Hanna: the story of Anatole Morel, Vincent's grandfather. While Vincent's gradual understanding of Hanna's history builds empathic identification and solidarity, the discovery of his grandfather's past is destructive of individual and family identity. Faced with the silence of his parents and grandmother, Vincent, in the last chapters of the novel, locates a 'black notebook' which is Anatole's diary of the last months of his life from 23 October 1943 to 2 September 1944. Unlike Hanna's story of persecution told in fragments, Anatole's story of collaboration is presented in full in diary format, allowing the voice of the perpetrator to answer that of his victim over fifty years later. It is to Szac's credit that the fictionalised entries build a portrait not of a monster but rather of an individual seduced by the authoritarian values of the Vichy regime and the excesses of his superiors, historical figures Paul Touvier and Joseph Lécussan.[42] Devotion to family, a desire for stability, a belief in the rule of law and a limited intellect all offer some form of explanation for Anatole Morel's wartime choices which end with suicide. As an alternate war story to that of Hanna, the neighbour whom he denounces for the additional room her small apartment would give his family, Anatole incarnates national culpability and shame.

The effects of such war narratives on the adolescent narrator are two-fold and can be read as incarnating a civic memory of the Second World War in two respects. Firstly, the re-emergence of such war narratives enables Vincent to reflect on his personal responsibility and to attempt some form of emotional reparation. This begins as a rejection of his family past and flight from Lyon to become homeless for a period in Avignon. This period of isolation enables him to understand that he must take responsibility for his family past. This entails accepting a direct confrontation with his family history and refusing to reproduce the same heavy silence as his predecessors. Demonstrating his solidarity with others beyond the family, Vincent ends the novel reunited with Hanna who absolves him of culpability for the crimes of his grandfather. Secondly, the novel proposes a cross-cultural reflection on the experiences of persecution, triggered by the narrative revelation of the Second World War. When Vincent works as an activities coordinator in an ethnically mixed suburb of Lyon, he comes into contact with another war story of persecution; that of Farid who, when asked to mime the role of a *maman* as part of a game of charades, enacts his mother's distress as a forced migrant: 'Le groupe s'est mis à chahuter, personne ne trouvait la réponse, les gosses en avaient assez. Je ne pouvais pas détacher mes yeux de cet enfant qui, pour interpréter une maman, mimait la détresse, la violence, la fuite, sans doute l'exil.'[43] In this scene, the novel makes an explicit link between the wartime persecution of Jewish families in France and present-day atrocities where the rights and lives of children are ignored. In the words of Mitzi Myers, such lessons for 'humane living' are a powerful tool. In *Un lourd silence*, this episode underscores how a rediscovered French past can act as a catalyst for reflection on global events, stimulating identification with displaced children as one of the most vulnerable groups in such situations.

Un lourd silence can, therefore, be read as offering a more complex and morally ambiguous set of war narratives to Boudet's *Mon prof est un espion*. Children and adolescents are investigators (Vincent) and victims (Myrha). There is no safe distance from memory and, as Szac points out, the repercussions of the past haunt the present. Working through memory is key to the novel and Vincent's need to know, understand and take responsibility for the past brings dangers both for his sense of self and for the national war narratives with which he has been educated. The resistance epic is transformed into a national tale of shame, culpability and betrayal. However, the novel offers the young reader reassurance, both in the form of a reconciliatory ending, Hanna and Vincent reunited in full knowledge of each other's family past, and in the universalist lessons such war memories might offer contemporary generations. These centre on the importance of empathic identification with present-day child victims of violence and greater sensitivity towards the human costs of discrimination and persecution. In the last children's crime novel examined in this chapter, such reassurance is hardly possible as a young adult's narrative of persecution carries few redemptive possibilities.

Romain Slocombe's *Qui se souvient de Paula?* (2008) was published in Editions Syros' Rat noir collection, a series marketed as providing a bridge between children's crime fiction and adult fiction.[44] In its very title, the novel asks the adolescent reader to speculate on questions of memory: Which memories of the Second World War do we retain? Who have we remembered and who have we forgotten? Why should we remember? The novel is set on two temporal planes: firstly, the years 1942–43 which follow the life and almost certain death of twenty-year-old Paula Karlinski. This era is reconstructed via Paula's letters and journal entries, a Jewish literature student in Paris whose narrative is reminiscent of the style and tone of Hélène Berr's successful *Journal*.[45] The second time frame is the narrative present, July 1997, and the quest of the aged Jacques Masaran, Paula's wartime sweetheart, to discover more about her life and death. This is a quest animated by the impossible hope that she may have returned from the camps. This quest leads him to track down the man who began the chain of denunciation which leads to Paula's death. The novel ends with Maxime Thévenot's murder, still resident in the building where he committed his crime, and Jacques's suicide on the door step of Paula's former apartment as he awaits the police, fully reconciled to the consequences of the retributive justice he has enacted.

The structure and form of the novel is intentionally fractured, with several narrators and timeframes, and the use of first and third-person narration preventing any univocal narration of the past. In addition, letters, journal entries, and even internet postings, inscribe a plethora of generic material into the whole, some of which are presented in italicised texts, others not. The effect of such narrative experimentation is twofold: by placing past and present side by side, such temporally split narration disrupts, what Sue Vice describes as, 'a teleological and back shadowing view of history, and complicat[es] the precedence of either mode'.[46] It draws the two time frames into dialogue and creates an interleaving effect which challenges a simplistic equation of the present explaining the past. Secondly, such a fractured text represents textually the effects of trauma as an inability to separate past from present, the one implicated in the other. In the last pages of the novel, the time frames merge in Jacques's distressed imagination until the past finally suffuses and overwhelms the present.

Unlike *Mon prof est un espion* and *Un lourd silence,* the Second World War and Jewish persecution in *Qui se souvient de Paula?* are reconstructed via a narrator/protagonist who is a victim of Jewish persecution and is fully immersed in events. The first part of novel, 'La Lettre', is Paula's extended epistolary account of her life as a Jew in occupied France in late 1942. In the second part, 'Le Retour', dated January 1943, an extra-diegetic narrator continues the narrative of Paula's persecution and eventual capture. The third part, 'Le Lac', set in July 1997, follows Jacques Masaran's response to an internet posting, posing the question who remembers Paula Karlinski? In his privileging of the historic past (two-thirds of the text is devoted to this time frame), Slocombe demonstrates his commitment to an empathic evocation of daily life for the Jewish population. This begins with the intensification of deprivation and discrimination to reach a crescendo in the depiction of control, surveillance and full-scale persecution.

Narrated via the perspective of Paula, a young woman from a highly educated French-Jewish family, the war period is presented as an era of erosion in basic human rights for Jews, a fact which is presented as of little interest to the general population. Paula has to contend with her exclusion from university studies; reduced access to food, transport and fuel, and then hiding and flight to the non-occupied zone where Protestant escape networks help her find refuge with a farming family. As in *Un lourd silence*, the focus, in both first and third-person narration, is on the collusion of the French authorities, individually and collectively, in such escalating persecution. Paula has to contend with informants, such as the apparently well-meaning French gentleman who gives up his seat for her on the train to Paris but only in order to mark her out as a Jew for the police checks later on in the journey. In similar *roman noir* fashion, Paula encounters figures, such as her former classmate Jérôme Naudet, who plays all sides in the war, providing information to the Gestapo, the Gaullists and operating a lucrative black market in drugs trafficking. Opening with a quotation from André Héléna's *Le Bon Dieu s'en fout*, Slocombe's aesthetic vision and tone have much in common with the fictional universe of Héléna's wartime novels, such as *Les Salauds ont la vie dure!* or *Le Festival des macchabées,* where resistance heroism is roundly rejected.[47] Like these earlier *noir* narratives, Slocombe's novel projects a morally dark vision of occupation onto the dilapidated buildings, rain-soaked streets and lugubrious alley ways of a labyrinthine Paris. However, rather than a compromised resistance, memories of Jewish persecution become the primary means of understanding the arbitrary violence and distress of life under Vichy and German rule.

The innovation of the novel is to examine the repercussions of such a forgotten life on present-day relations and identities. Fifty years later, the past resurfaces as an internet appeal for information concerning Paula Karlinski and to which Jacques Masaran responds. Meeting Pierrette Pons in her retirement home overlooking the still lake which gives the third section its name, Jacques is obliged to consider many buried memories from the past. These include Pierrette's wartime past as a neighbour of the Karlinski family and who is wracked with guilt that she gave away the location of Paula and her father's hiding place in Paris under torture. Jacques too confesses to his feelings of inadequacy at choosing not to resist once he had reached the safety of London. What the remembered figure of Paula generates in both protagonists is a renewed sense of survivor guilt as both have been unable to process the past, burdened as they are with feelings of shame.

In sharp contrast to *Mon prof est un espion* and *Un lourd silence*, *Qui se souvient de Paula?* does not revolve around educating child/adolescent investigators but rather presents the traumatic impact of the past on an older generation and their ethical responsibility to pass on their wartime past to others. Paula's worldly goods, handed over to Jacques by Pierrette in a battered suitcase, come to stand in metonymically for the life cut short by persecution and extermination and their joint responsibility to understand the circumstances of her death. For Pierrette and Jacques form part of a chain of testimony which functions as the narrative thread bringing the past and present into contact. The first witness is Paula herself, via her journal contained in the small suitcase and which we eventually learn will be published by Jacques. The second witness is the Holocaust survivor, Myriam Halpern, a school friend and fellow Jew, who encounters Paula at Drancy and travels with her to Auschwitz. She calls Jacques to her bedside in June 1945 at the Hotel Lutétia as she lies dying. This testimony, woven into the last pages of the novel as Jacques faces the man who denounced Pierrette, acts as a form of delayed transmission and represents the eruption of the past into the present. The last link in the chain of testimony is Jacques who annotates Paula's letters and journal and sends them to Presses Universitaires de France before his murderous encounter with Maxime Thévenot. This material, which we have indeed been reading, stands in as a mode of cultural memory, a form of posthumous recognition which underscores the importance of disseminating such war memories beyond family or closed social networks. In his capacity as a university lecturer, Jacques represents the ethical responsibility of the educational establishment to animate history, giving it life and significance for future generations.

The urgency of this ethical responsibility to confront the past is made clear by Slocombe in his representation of perpetration. Paula's experiences of persecution have, as their darkly inverted other, the justifications of Thévenot whom Jacques confronts in his apartment surrounded by fascist war memorabilia. This puts the reader in no doubt as to Slocombe's views on the need for continuing vigilance in the face of modern-day fascism and anti-Semitism. Thévenot's narrative of perpetration is not, as in the case of Szac's perpetrator, given scope for development. Set alongside Myriam Halpern's deathbed testimony, his extreme anti-Semitism is presented as delusional but damaging. The factual riposte to such ignorance is delivered at the start of the narrative in Slocombe's decision to begin his novel with a reproduction of Circulaire no. 173-42 of 13 July 1942 in which local authorities were asked to prepared for the 16 July 1942 *rafle du Vélodrome d'Hiver*. The dehumanising language of the document; its explicit instructions to remain immune to the appeals of those to be arrested, and the information given on the French authorities' decision to include children under sixteen, prepare the reader to condemn figures such as Thévenot. Paula's story becomes emblematic of many other Jewish stories which will never be told; for whom there is no journal or letters with which to mark their passing. The novel can be read as a fictionalised 'memorial book', as much about collective as individual remembrance.[48]

Qui se souvient de Paula? reaffirms the ethical imperative to remember central to *Un lourd silence* and more elliptically present in *Mon prof est un espion*. It imagines Jewish children and young people lost in the tumult of war and calls upon the reader to identify and empathise with their plight. The past is not irrecoverable in *Qui se souvient de Paula?* and retains a power that, in *roman noir* fashion, disrupts present-day relations. The ending is not one of reassurance for the young reader: Paula will never return; Jacques commits a murder which does not represent a coming to terms with the past; and a bloody revenge takes place which will not be understood. As the policeman called to the murder scene in the last lines speaks into this walkie-talkie: 'Restez chez vous, madame, 'y a rien à voir',[49] it would seem that, yet again as in wartime, nothing has been seen in the apartment block; no one wants to speak up and nobody remains to tell the story. However, the novel positions itself to offer the adolescent reader a memory of the war years that makes much of its hybrid status as children's crime fiction and historical fiction. Ending the novel with an annotated bibliography, Slocombe gives details of the real-life model for Paula Karlinski, Louise Jacobson, and sets out the authentic materials on which the narrative is based. In its precise charting of the mechanisms of deportation and use of eye-witness accounts, the novel confirms the importance of building a cultural memory of the past informed by extensive research and committed to the humanist values of solidarity, compassion and respect for others.

Conclusion

The three novels which have been discussed in this chapter confirm the prevalence of narratives of Jewish persecution and extermination in recent war fiction for younger readers. This pattern conforms to broader trends in contemporary cultural production, with a number of war films, fictions and autobiographical writings pivoting on memories of Jewish persecution and French state collusion in the Holocaust.[50] The recognition of such war memories within the political and cultural establishment has reinforced the legitimacy of such a narrativisation of the

Second World War. As Jacques Chirac stressed in his 16 July 1995 speech, the role of the national community today is to 'témoigner encore et encore. Reconnaître les fautes du passé, et les fautes commises par l'Etat. Ne rien occulter des heures sombres de notre histoire … '.[51] However, the reframing of the past which this chapter has identified in children's crime fictions can also be attributed to broader shifts in the French memorial landscape. As *Un lourd silence* makes evident, memories of the Second World War can allow authors to make cross-cultural and transhistorical connections which generate reflection on present-day social violence and exile. None of this is to refute the specificity of French experiences of the Second World War but rather to consider the potential for such legacies to inform younger readers about the world around them. For children's crime fiction suggests that the Second World War may be entering a new phase of memory, one which sees its integration into an inclusive civic memory of the recent past. From this perspective, the Second World War may have reached a level of acceptance as social history which augurs well for the maturation of public debate. Indeed, it may be the case that interest in the war period will diminish as the social demand for greater engagement with contested memories of decolonisation increases. Memories of the Second World War could be mobilised very differently in the reframing of a colonial past and discussion of sensitive issues, such as the use of torture by the French army or national responses to post-war immigration.

Finally, the crime fictions for younger readers examined in this chapter are emblematic of a more general shift in war fictions in France from politically and ideologically inflected war narratives towards an immersion in an affective memory where individual tragedy can take precedent over critical historical representation. The wounded or dead child as an emotive figure of identification is a powerful narrative tool in these children's war fictions but also poses ethical questions over the extent to which 'storying war' can adversely shape our understandings of war. There is always the danger that the dramatisation of a child's loss may bring emotional overload and a loss of historical contextualisation. However, it can be argued that the child should be read more figuratively in such crime fictions as a repository of cultural memory and the primary vector through which memory is transmitted. This is not memory via family history or national commemoration but memory via assumption of civic responsibility towards some of the most vulnerable members of society. From this optic, fictionalised children and children's fiction become privileged carriers of memory. They are able to promote the value of intergenerational caring and the benefits of carrying hopeful negotiations with the past into the future.

Notes

1 'France, the home of the Enlightenment and human rights, a land of welcome and asylum, France, that day, committed an irreparable act'. See www.fr.wikisource.org/wiki/discours_prononce_lors_des_commemorations_de_la_rafle_du_Vel_d'Hiv (accessed 8 February 2012) for a full transcript of this speech.

2 See Chapter 5, 'Une mémoire apaisée? de Jacques Chirac à Nicolas Sarkozy (de 1995 à nos jours)', in Olivier Wieviorka, *La Mémoire désunie: le souvenir politique des années sombres de la Libération à nos jours* (Paris: Editions du Seuil, 2010), pp. 237–74, for an overview and analysis of such developments.

3 Olivier Wieviorka, in *La Mémoire désunie*, makes much of the troubled wartime history of François Mitterrand and the extent to which it cast doubt on his ability to adjudicate on French wartime legacies. Richard Golsan develops a similar thesis in *Vichy's Afterlife: History and Counterhistory in Postwar France* (Lincoln: Nebraska University Press, 2001) and identifies a number of post-war French leaders whose ambivalent wartime histories have left them compromised in the eyes of the French public.

4 Wieviorka, *La Mémoire désunie*, p. 22.

5 This is evident in the vogue for films representing the Second World War and its legacies, in direct and indirect ways. These include: *Un secret* (2007. dir. Claude Miller), *L'Armée du crime* (2008, dir. Robert Guédiguian), *La Rafle* (2010, dir. Rose Bosch), *Elle s'appelait Sarah* (2010, dir. Gilles Paquet-Brenner) and *La Question humaine* (2007, dir. Nicolas Klotz and Elisabeth Perceval).

6 Alexandre Jardin, *Des gens très bien* (Paris: Bernard Grasset, 2010), p. 29 (If we are not responsible for the actions of our fathers and grandfathers … we remain responsible for our perspective on the past). In this autobiographical fiction, Alexandre Jardin confronts the family legacy of his grandfather, Jean Jardin, and his wartime role as chief secretary to Pierre Laval at the time of the *rafle du Vélodrome d'Hiver*.

7 In the conclusion to *La Mémoire désunie*, Olivier Wieviorka comments on the potential for the Second World War to act as a key element in the civic education of younger generations, above all combating contemporary manifestations of racism and fanaticism. See *La Mémoire désunie*, p. 288.

8 Jean-Philippe Mathy, 'Transmission problems: memory, community and the republican idea in contemporary France', *Journal of European Studies*, 35:2 (2005), 237–45 (238).

9 Mathy, 'Transmission problems', 238.

10   Lucie Aubrac, *La Résistance expliquée à mes petits-enfants* (Paris: Editions du Seuil, 2000).

11   Aubrac, *La Résistance expliquée à mes petits-enfants*, p. 54 (you fought and you won out over hatred, racism and violence. If we had to, we would be ready to act as you did).

12   A. Bonifacio, P. Maréchal, *Histoire de France: Cours moyen 1ère année* (Paris: Hachette, 1964), p. 119.

13   It is significant that teaching the Second World War is embedded within a human rights discourse and surely reflects upon prosecution of war criminals in France and elsewhere in the 1990s. I am indebted to Solange Pierrat-Dané for access to the current French history curriculum programmes at primary and secondary levels.

14   Written paper, Baccalauréat Général, session 2010, Histoire-Géographie, Séries L et ES, pp. 3–8.

15   Mitzi Myers, 'Storying war: an overview', in Elizabeth Goodenough and Andrea Immel (eds), *Under Fire: Childhood in the Shadow of War* (Detroit, MI: Wayne State University Press, 2008), pp. 19–27.

16   Myers, 'Storying war: an overview', p. 19.

17   It is interesting in this respect to consider the Imperial War Museum's exhibition 'Once upon a wartime: classic war stories for children', 11 February to 30 October 2011. The exhibition took visitors on a journey through conflicts from the First World War to the present day depicted in five children's novels, three of which were devoted to the Second World War. The exhibition was organised thematically and made use of expert interpretation and examples of relevant objects from particular conflicts. There was a particular focus on children's experiences of civilian displacement and exile (two of the five themes were separation and survival). However, the Holocaust was absent from the spaces and texts devoted to the Second World War. This may have been due to the largely British perspective on childhood during the Second World War in the exhibition, exemplified in the figure of the evacuee.

18   Myers, 'Storying war: an overview', p. 26.

19   See Hamida Bosmajian, *Sparing the Child: Grief and the Unspeakable in Youth Literature about Nazism and the Holocaust* (London: Routledge, 2002).

20   Michel Quint, *Effroyables Jardins* (Paris: Editions Joëlle Losfeld, 2000). The market for cross-writing is evident here in the Editions Pocket Jeunesse 2003 edition which includes a pedagogical dossier aimed at secondary school children.

21   Philippe Grimbert, *Un secret* (Paris: Editions Grasset et Fasquelle, 2004). This novel won the Prix Goncourt des lycéens in 2004, voted upon by secondary school children.

22   Tatiana de Rosnay, *Sarah's Key* (London: John Murray, 2006). A bilingual French-English writer, de Rosnay had written eight novels in French

before *Sarah's Key*, her first in English. Translated into French in 2007 as *Elle s'appelait Sarah*, it has sold over two million copies worldwide and was made into a major French film in 2010, starring Kristin Scott-Thomas.

23 For a short history of French children's crime fiction, see Eliane Dufour, 'Le Roman policier pour la jeunesse: quelques repères historiques', in Françoise Ballanger (ed.), *Enquête sur le roman policier pour la jeunesse* (Paris/Mairie de Paris: La Joie par les Livres/Paris Bibliothèques Editions, 2003), pp. 82–95.

24 Dufour, 'Le Roman policier pour la jeunesse', p. 82 (a literature under surveillance).

25 For an overview of the changes in children's crime fiction collections in France since the mid-1980s, see Françoise Ballanger, Sylvie Kha and Alain Regnault, 'L'Evolution des collections depuis 1986', in Ballanger (ed.), *Enquête sur le roman policier pour la jeunesse*, pp. 100–32.

26 See Raymond Perrin, *Histoire du polar jeunesse: romans et bandes dessinées* (Paris: L'Harmattan, 2011), pp. 156–62, for a discussion of the inroads crime fiction has made into the French classroom.

27 See Béatrice Nicodème, *Ami, entends-tu … ?* (Paris: Gulf Stream Editeur, 2008), which focuses on an adolescent protagonist in the Resistance in Nantes in 1943; Liliane Korb and Laurence Lefèvre, *L'Etrange Affaire Plumet* (Paris: Flammarion, 1996) has a present-day child investigator unearthing memories of collaboration in his local village; Jean-Hugues Oppel's *Le Feu au lac* (Paris: Albin Michel, 2000) takes place in Switzerland and exposes the collaborationist past of local dignitaries; Jean-Paul Nozière, *Les Assassins du cercle rouge* (Paris: Flammarion, 1997) centres on two child investigators and their discovery of wartime documents and contemporary neo-Nazi networks; and Thierry Crifo's *La Dernière Séquence* (Paris: Albin Michel, 2000) builds its intrigue around the history of a local cinema and its connections to wartime collaboration.

28 Didier Daeninckx, *Galadio* (Paris: Editions Larousse, 2010) is published with a pedagogical dossier. It would appear that both authors and editors are now aware of the commercial opportunities offered by crime fictions that speak to prescribed school curriculum topics. For an analysis of this development, see Annie Collovald, 'Le Roman policier à l'école des pédagogues', in Françoise Ballanger (ed.), *Enquête sur le roman policier pour la jeunesse*, pp. 58–63.

29 All references will be to the following edition: Robert Boudet, *Mon prof est un espion* (Paris: Casterman, 2010).

30 See Perrin, *Histoire du polar jeunesse*, p. 158.

31 The use of Buchenwald as a destination for deported Jewish families is surprising and historically inaccurate. This could be attributed to the secondary importance of this plot element in comparison to the story of the child survivor, Louis/David, and his identity quest.

32 Boudet, *Mon prof est un espion*, p. 52 (for the moment, it's like reading Hebrew).
33 Bosmajian, *Sparing the Child*, p. xiv.
34 Boudet, *Mon prof est un espion*, p. 82 (the abominable end).
35 Boudet, *Mon prof est un espion*, p. 88 ('It is important to know who you are ...' said Natalie. Louis Forestier sighs. 'And when you discover that you aren't who you thought you were').
36 Szac, *Un lourd silence*, p. 6 (I wrote this book because I am convinced of one thing: each of us needs to know where we come from. There can be no freedom or future without memory of the past, without a history of our origins. We are not guilty or accountable for the actions of those who went before us, but we must know).
37 All references will be to the following edition: Murielle Szac, *Un lourd silence* (Paris: Editions Gallimard, 2009), collection Karactères.
38 Szac, *Un lourd silence*, p. 43 (resisted without thinking about it. It was as natural for him as it was for others to do nothing).
39 Szac, *Un lourd silence*, pp. 47–8 (In July 1941, it was a French civil servant who stamped my identity card in red with the word 'Jew' and entered my details onto a register. Like a plague carrier. In October 1940, it was French law that imposed a separate status upon Jews ... Forbidden, forbidden, forbidden, everything is forbidden. And it was the French government that decided this. The cousins who brought me to Lyon had a hat shop on rue des Pierres-Plantés. It was confiscated and handed over legally to a respectable Frenchman. And in the summer of 1942, when thousands of Jews were being rounded up in the Guillotière district and in the whole of Lyon, it was the French police who came for them to send them to the slaughterhouse).
40 The novel is based on local history as Szac integrates the real-life figures of Claude Gutmann, a member of the local Jewish scouting organisation, and Abbé Glasberg, of the group Amitiés chriétiennes, into her story of the survival of a number of children from the Vénissieux camp. See Szac, *Un lourd silence*, pp. 96–9.
41 Pierre refers to the *rafle du Vélodrome d'Hiver* in Paris as if to reinforce the extent of national culpability, Szac, *Un lourd silence*, p. 66.
42 The narrative technique of presenting the collaborating father via his diary entries echoes the technique of earlier *mode rétro* texts, such as Marie Chaix's *Les Lauriers du lac de Constance* (Paris: Gallimard, 1974).
43 Szac, *Un lourd silence*, p. 90 (The group began to mess around, nobody knew the answer, the kids had had enough. I couldn't take my eyes off this child who, in order to act out the role of a mummy, imitated distress, violence, flight, and probable exile).
44 Romain Slocombe writes adult crime fiction and has a personal interest in the history of the Second World War. His grandfather was the British historian, journalist and political commentator, George Slocombe, who

broadcast for the BBC during the war years. All references will be to the only edition of the text to date: Slocombe, *Qui se souvient de Paula?* (Paris: Editions Syros, 2008).

45 Hélène Berr's *Journal* was published in 2008 to critical acclaim. She bequeathed her wartime journal to her sweetheart, Jean Morawiecki who, like Jacques Masaran in *Qui se souvient de Paula?*, was committed to making her wartime story known more widely. In the bibliography which ends the novel, Slocombe pays tribute to Louise Jacobson, a seventeen-year-old Jewish *lycée* student in Paris, whose letters he draws on, sometimes verbatim, in the sections devoted to Paula's narration.

46 Sue Vice, *Children Writing the Holocaust* (London: Palgrave/Macmillan, 2004), p. 12.

47 See Chapter 1 of this volume for a discussion of André Héléna's war fictions.

48 The term 'memorial book ' is taken from Sue Vice, *Children Writing the Holocaust*, p. 163.

49 Slocombe, *Qui se souvient de Paula?*, p. 259 (stay inside madam, there is nothing to see).

50 This is evident in best-selling popular studies of France produced by foreign writers, such as Graham Robb's *Parisians: An Adventure History of Paris* (London: Picador, 2010). In the section devoted to 'occupation', Robb tells the story of Paris during the war years through the eyes of Jewish children, drawing heavily on eye-witness testimony. See pp. 269–84.

51 'To testify again and again. To recognise the errors of the past, state errors. To hide nothing that relates to the darkest hours of our history'. See www.fr.wikisource.org/wiki/discours_prononce_lors_des_commemorations_de_la_rafle_du_Vel_d'Hiv (accessed 8 February 2012).

Conclusion

Memories past, present and future

L'homme est avant tout mémoire, qui lui explique son passé et l'éclaire sur les choix de son avenir, bref lui dessine son destin.[1]

In his introduction to the *Yale French Studies* volume devoted to multidirectional memory in post-war French and francophone culture, Michael Rothberg outlines a model of cultural or collective memory. It is one that focuses upon the 'knotted' intersections of histories and memories produced in contemporary memory cultures. In this model, Rothberg advocates rethinking memory as acts of remembrance defined by social frameworks anchored in the nation-state. He proposes instead a fluid model of memory networks that allow multiple and multi-layered points of contact between past events to resurface. As Rothberg asserts, 'memory emerges from unexpected, multidirectional encounters – encounters between diverse pasts and a conflictual present, to be sure, but also between different agents or catalysts of memory'.[2] In this book, memories of the Second World War have been examined via encounters with crime fiction, a popular agent of memory that has connected with the wartime past across decades, generations and communities of readers. What this study has demonstrated is both the cultural specifics of crime fiction's interaction with the Second World War (its narrative templates, its thematic preoccupations) and the broader patterning of memory that crime fiction renders visible. This popular patterning of memory is not one that always correlates to Henry Rousso's model of the Vichy syndrome. For if the Vichy syndrome rightly remains a landmark study of the presence of the Vichy past in French public and political life, crime fiction emphasises different circuits of memory, informed by more diffuse social and cultural processes of remembrance. These popular circuits of memory can help enhance our understanding of cultural memories of the war years and their evolution in France in three key respects.

Firstly, the crime fiction discussed in this study has confirmed a movement away from politically and ideologically inflected representations of the Second World War towards narratives preoccupied with the moral dilemmas of remembrance. In the late 1940s and 1950s, crime fictions about the Second World War tended to be informed by personal experience and to concentrate on the political repercussions of war, occupation and liberation. These novels emphasised the ideological interests at stake in promoting certain war narratives and their exploitation by sectarian groupings. Such a war narrative can be traced in the work of the *roman noir* novelists examined in Chapter 1 who constructed counter-histories of resistance with which to contest the epic stories of heroism endorsed by the ruling political elites. In contrast, in the 1980s and 1990s, this concern with the factionalism and the political legacies of war had largely been superseded by narratives which depicted second-generation protagonists grappling with the actions and motivations of parents and grandparents who lived through the war. This leads, as Chapter 5 demonstrates, to an emotive confrontation with a different set of war experiences, above all those centred on Jewish persecution, deportation and extermination. The overriding impulse, as dramatised in such fictions, is not to settle scores with former adversaries but to explore familial and generational legacies of war that impact upon present-day French identities. The lost Jewish child is a particularly resonant symbol of war suffering in this context and her or his centrality to narratives of war is intended to generate empathic identification on the part of the reader. It is this evolution in memories of the Second World War in France – from a political to an affective engagement with memory – that crime fiction maps so persuasively.

Secondly, the crime novels in this volume have demonstrated the role of popular culture in shaping, as well as reflecting, cultural memories of the Second World War in France. Since the 1970s, French crime fiction has been at the forefront of popularising new historical research on France and the Second World War. This trend can be traced in relation to the phenomenon of wartime collaboration, minimised in the immediate aftermath of war but brought back into public consciousness with the publication of research that highlighted the varied and multiple forms collaboration took and its legitimisation by and within the Vichy state. As the novels studied in Chapter 3 prove, this expansive and systemic model of collaboration was adopted by a number of French crime writers in the 1980s and 1990s and led to popular reformulation of the scope, reach and significance of collaboration. The movement to build upon the research momentum of historians can also be identified in the development of meticulously researched crime fiction devoted to the *univers concentrationnaire*. The novels of Thierry Jonquet, Gérard Delteil and Konop examined in Chapter 4 allow for an interrogation of hybrid crime fictions – simultaneously historical chronicle and imaginative reconstruction. The novels selected probe crime fiction's role as a cultural narrative able to mediate growing public interest in cases of crimes against humanity and the difficulties facing successor generations confronted with often incomplete histories of the wartime past. In Didier Daeninckx's *Meurtres pour mémoire* (1984) examined in Chapter 3, these transmission problems take the form of a multi-directional memory of French wartime collusion in the persecution of the Jews and the brutal police repression of a demonstration in Paris on 17 October 1961 at the height of the Algerian War.

Lastly, the crime novels examined in this book have reasserted the distinctive contribution of fiction to debates on the evolution of memories of the Second World War in France.[3] What has emerged over the course of this study is a modulated cultural history of war memories which emphasises continuity rather than rupture. There is continuity in themes and preoccupations, for example the post-war political manipulations of a resistance legacy or the suffering and hardship of life under occupation, as well as continuity of production; research shows a steady flow of publications over the post-war period with peaks and troughs which can be attributed to the visibility of memory discourses of war more generally in the public domain. Indeed, the patterns of publication in French crime fiction about the Second World War correspond imperfectly to the chronological modelling of post-war memory outlined in Rousso's *Vichy syndrome*. For example, there is no period of silence or repression of the darker histories of the war years as is commonly asserted about the 1950s and 1960s. Rather, as Chapter 2 demonstrates, crimes against the Jewish community are not forgotten during a period of consolidation for a Gaullist myth of resistance. They enter a number of crime novels in displaced forms that suggest conflicted responses to French guilt and complicity in the Holocaust. It can even be argued that French crime novelists have appropriated the Second World War as a historical laboratory of sorts in which to test out questions of national identity and civic responsibility. As Chapter 5 argues, this can be read against a reconfiguration of twentieth-century war memories in France in the 1990s and

2000s and the privileging of a human rights discourse that advocates an ethics of responsibility for a new generation of French citizens.

In his chapter devoted to the changing landscape of French memory and the Second World War, Philippe Buton identifies a decisive break, 'a revolution in memory', for France in 1994.[4] For Buton, this occurred following revelations of President François Mitterrand's Vichy past, thereby ending 'the fiction, carefully maintained by all presidents and all governments since the Liberation, of France's role as the innocent victim'.[5] A dual vision emerged of France as morally tainted by its Vichy past but also committed to the Republican and humanist values associated with those who opposed and eventually defeated such a regime. For Buton, writing in 2007, 'slowly and progressively assimilated, the memory of the Second World War has been pacified' to be replaced by another war memory that nags at the historical or civic consciousness: the Algerian War.[6] The crime fiction studied here testifies to this step change in memory during the 1990s. As the bibliography to this volume reveals, many of the novels explored here were republished in the 1990s and 2000s, indicating a resurgence of interest in often antagonistic war narratives. This trend supports Buton's thesis that there has been an opening-up of memory that has translated into a greater readiness to acknowledge the light and the shades of the wartime past. Yet, the notion of a pacified wartime past is problematic as an end point. As Rothberg's model of multidirectional memory suggests, it is not possible to predict the knotted histories which may be reactivated in the future, particularly as the French wars of decolonisation loom large in the memory transmission of second- and third-generation North-African immigrants to France. It may well be that memories of the Second World War persist, albeit in new and unexpected constellations that intersect with different historical periods and collective trajectories. As Jean Cassou wrote in 1953 in *La Mémoire courte*, if memory explains our past, it also informs our future choices and destiny. The contribution of popular forms, such as crime fiction, is to illuminate that past and to continue to offer powerful cultural interventions that shape the landscape of memory.

Notes

1   Jean Cassou, *La Mémoire courte* (Paris: Librairie Arthème Fayard, 2001), p. 7 (man is, above all else, memory; this explains his past and clarifies his future choices, in sum it determines his destiny).
2   Michael Rothberg, 'Introduction: between memory and memory, from

lieux de mémoire to *noeuds de mémoire'*, *Yale French Studies*, 118–19 (2011), 3–12 (9).

3   See the contributions to a special issue of *French Cultural Studies*, 22:3 (2011) devoted to re-examining fictional narratives of the occupation. In her introduction, Margaret Atack states that the aim of the volume is to 'offer a differently inflected view of the Occupation narrative by approaching "other stories" from very different angles, by presenting stories that have not yet been told and by examining otherness in very new contexts' (184).

4   Philippe Buton, 'Occupation, liberation, purges: the changing landscape of French memory', in Andrew Knapp (ed.), *Uncertain Foundation: France at the Liberation, 1944–47* (Basingstoke: Palgrave, 2007), pp. 234–49 (p. 245).

5   Buton, 'Occupation, liberation, purges', p. 245.

6   Buton, 'Occupation, liberation, purges', p. 247.

Bibliography

Primary texts

The listing of primary texts provides details of all the French crime novels about the Second World War referenced in this study. The most recent editions are listed here.

Amoz, Claude. *L'Ancien Crime* (Paris: Payot et Rivages, 1999)

Arnaud, Georges-Jean. *L'Antizyklon des atroces* (Paris: EJL, 2001)

Arnaud, Georges-Jean. *Maudit Blood* (Paris: Editions du Rocher, 1998)

Arnaud, Georges-Jean. *Spoliation* (Paris: Fleuve noir, 2000)

Bialot, Joseph. *La Nuit du souvenir* (Paris: Gallimard, 2010)

Boudet, Robert. *Mon prof est un espion* (Paris: Casterman, 2010)

Cayre, Hannelore. *Toiles de maître* (Paris: Editions Métailié, 2005)

Chaboud, Jack. *Le Tronc de la veuve* (Paris: Le Passage, 2003)

Couturier, Hélène. *Sarah (*Paris: Payot and Rivages, 1999)

Crifo, Thierry. *La Dernière Séquence* (Paris: Albin Michel, 2000)

Daeninckx, Didier. *Galadio* (Paris: Editions Larousse, 2010)

Daeninckx, Didier. *La Mort n'oublie personne* (Paris: Gallimard, 1989)

Daeninckx, Didier, *Mémoire noire* (Paris: Gallimard, 2010), including *Meurtres pour mémoire*

Daeninckx, Didier. *Missak* (Paris: Perrin, 2009)

Daeninckx, Didier. *Murder in Memoriam*, trans. Liz Heron (London: Serpent's Tail, 1991)

Delteil, Gérard. *KZ retour vers l'enfer* (Paris: Editions Métailié, 1998)

Delteil, Gérard. *Mort d'un satrape rouge* (Paris: Métailié, 1998)

Didelot, Francis. *Dernier Matin* (Paris: Librairie des Champs-Elysées, 1977)

Errer, Emmanuel. *Un detour par l'enfer* (Paris: Fleuve noir, 1991)

Geffray, Stéphane. *Les Teutons flingueurs* (Paris: Editions Baleine, 1999)

Héléna, André. *Le Festival des macchabées* (Paris: Editions E-Dite, 2001)

Héléna, André. *Les Clients du Central Hôtel* (Paris: Editions E-Dite, 2000)

Héléna, André. *Les Salauds ont la vie dure!* (Paris: Editions E-Dite, 2001)

Bibliography

Jonquet, Thierry. *Les Orpailleurs* (Paris: Editions Gallimard, 2010)

Klotz, Claude. *Kobar* (Paris: Librairie générale française, 1994)

Konop. *Pas de kaddish pour Sylberstein* (Paris: Le Grand Livre du mois, 1997)

Korb, Liliane and Laurence Lefèvre. *L'Etrange Affaire Plumet* (Paris: Flammarion, 1996)

Malet, Léo. *120, rue de la gare* (Paris: Pocket, 2009)

Malet, Léo. *Léo Malet: Nestor Burma, Les Nouveaux Mystères de Paris I* (Paris: Editions Robert Laffont, 2006), including *Du rébecca rue des Rosiers* and *Des kilomètres de linceuls*

Mazarin, Jean. *Collabo-Song* (Cadeilhan: Zulma, 1998)

Meckert, Jean. *Nous avons les mains rouges* (Paris: Encrage, 1993)

Meckert, Jean. *Nous sommes tous des assassins* (Paris: Editions Joëlle Losfeld, 2008)

Mercader, Ramon. (Thierry Jonquet), *Du passé faisons table rase* (Paris: Albin Michel, 1982)

Monteilhet, Hubert. *Choc en retour* (Paris: Editions de Fallois, 2009)

Monteilhet, Hubert. *La Perte de vue: roman du temps de la Kollaboration* (Paris: Denoël, 1986)

Monteilhet, Hubert. *Hubert Monteilhet, Omnibus* (Paris: Editions de Fallois, 2008), including *Le Retour des cendres*

Monteilhet, Hubert. *Return from the Ashes*, trans. Tony White (London: Panther Books Ltd, 1965)

Morris, Gilles. *Assassin, mon frère* (Monaco: Editions du Rocher, 1990)

Nicodème, Béatrice. *Ami, entends-tu … ?* (Paris: Gulf Stream Editeur, 2008)

Nozière, Jean-Paul. *Les Assassins du cercle rouge* (Paris: Flammarion, 1997)

Oppel, Jean-Hugues. *Le Feu au lac* (Marseille: Rouge safran, 2009)

Pavloff, Franck. *Le Vent des fous* (Paris: Gallimard, 1993)

Pécherot, Patrick. *Boulevard des Branques* (Paris: Gallimard, 2005)

Simsolo, Noël. *Wazemmes* (Marseille: L'Ecailler du Sud, 2005)

Slocombe, Romain. *Qui se souvient de Paula?* (Paris: Editions Syros, 2008)

Szac, Murielle. *Un lourd silence* (Paris: Editions Gallimard, 2009)

Wagneur, Alain. *Homicide à bon marché* (Paris: Gallimard, 1996)

Secondary texts

Adler, Karen. *Jews and Gender in Liberation France* (Cambridge: Cambridge University Press, 2003)

Akoun, Nadine Rozenberg. 'L'Image du juif dans le roman policier français au XXème siècle: évolution et permanence' (Ph.D. dissertation, Université Paris VIII, 2004)

Amila, John [Jean Meckert]. *'Y a pas de bon dieu* (Paris: Gallimard, 1950)

Ashplant, T. G., Graham Dawson and Michael Roper (eds). *The Politics of War Memory and Commemoration* (London: Routledge, 2000)

Bibliography

Assmann, Jan. 'Collective memory and cultural identity', *New German Critique*, 65 (1995), 125–33

Atack, Margaret. 'Introduction', *French Cultural Studies*, 22:3 (2011), 183–5

Atack, Margaret. 'Representing the occupation in the novel of the 1950s: ne jugez pas', *Cincinnati Romance Review*, 29 (Fall 2010), 76–88

Aubrac, Lucie. *La Résistance expliquée à mes petits-enfants* (Paris: Editions du Seuil, 2000)

Ballanger, Françoise (ed.) *Enquête sur le roman policier pour la jeunesse* (Paris/Mairie de Paris: La Joie par les Livres/Paris Bibliothèques Editions, 2003)

Barthes, Roland. *S/Z* (Paris: Editions du Seuil, 1976)

Berkvam, Michael. *Writing the Story of France in World War II: Literature and Memory 1942-1958* (New Orleans, LA: University Press of the South, 2000)

Bosmajian, Hamida. *Sparing the Child: Grief and the Unspeakable in Youth Literature about Nazism and the Holocaust* (London: Routledge, 2002)

Buton, Philippe. 'Occupation, liberation, purges: the changing landscape of French memory', in Andrew Knapp (ed.), *Uncertain Foundation: France at the Liberation, 1944-47* (Basingstoke: Palgrave, 2007), pp. 234–49

Bracher, Nathan. 'Remembering the French resistance: ethics and poetics of the epic', *History and Memory*, 19:1 (2007), 39–67

Caldicott, Edric and Anne Fuchs (eds). *Cultural Memory: Essays on European Literature and History* (Bern: Peter Lang, 2003)

Callois, Roger. 'Puissances du roman', in *Approches de l'imaginaire* (Paris: Gallimard, 1974), pp. 177–205

Capdevila, Luc. 'Le mythe du guerrier et la construction sociale d'un éternel masculin après la guerre', *Revue française de psychanalyse*, 62:2 (1998), 607–723

Cassou, Jean. *La Mémoire courte* (Paris: Librairie Arthème Fayard, 2001)

Chandler, Raymond. 'The simple art of murder', reproduced in *Pearls are a Nuisance* (Harmondsworth: Penguin Books, 1966), pp. 181–99

Chaix, Marie. *Les Lauriers du lac de Constance* (Paris: Editions du Seuil, 1974)

Cheyette, Bryan. *Constructions of 'the Jew' in English Literature and Society: Racial Representations 1875-1945* (Cambridge: Cambridge University Press, 1993)

Conan, Eric and Henry Rousso. *Vichy, un passé qui ne passe pas* (Paris: Editions Fayard, 1994)

Confino, Alon. 'Memory and cultural history: problems of method', *The American Historical Review*, 102:5 (1997), 1386–1403

Confino, Alon. 'Remembering the Second World War, 1945–1965: narratives of victimhood and genocide', *Cultural Analysis*, 4 (2005), 46–75

Daeninckx, Didier. *La Mémoire longue, textes et images 1986-2008* (Paris: Le Cherche-Midi, 2008)

Daeninckx, Didier. *La Mort n'oublie personne* (Paris: Gallimard, 1989)

Bibliography

Deleuse, Robert. 'Petite histoire du roman noir français', *Les Temps modernes*, 595 (1997), 53–87

Deloux, Jean-Pierre. 'Blanche à filet rouges', *Polar*, 16 (1995), 2–31

Dhoukar, Nadia. 'Préface', *Léo Malet: Nestor Burma, Les Nouveaux Mystères de Paris II* (Paris: Editions Robert Laffont, 2006), pp. vii–xlvi

Emanuel, Michelle. *From Surrealism to Less-Exquisite Cadavers: Léo Malet and the Evolution of the French Roman Noir* (Amsterdam: Rodopi, 2006)

Erll, Astrid. 'Wars we have seen: literature as a medium of collective memory in the "age of extremes"', in Elena Lambert and Vita Fortunati (eds), *Memories and Representations of War: The Case of World War One and World War Two* (Amsterdam: Rodopi, 2009), pp. 27–43.

Evans, Martin. 'Opening up the battlefield: war studies and the cultural turn', *Journal of War and Culture Studies*, 1:1 2008, 47–51

Felman, Shoshana and Dori Laub. *Testimony: Crises of Witnessing in Literature, Psychoanalysis and History* (London: Routledge, 1992)

Forsdick, Charles. '"Direction les oubliettes de l'histoire": witnessing the past in the French polar', *French Cultural Studies*, 12:3 (2001), 333–50

Fulbrook, Mary. 'Patterns of Memory', in Katharina Hall and Kathryn N. Jones (eds), *Constructions of Conflict: Transmitting Memories of the Past in European Historiography, Culture and Media* (Bern: Peter Lang, 2011), pp. 17–33

Furst, Alan. *The World at Night* (London: HarperCollins Publishers, 1998)

Garcin, Jérôme. 'Jean Meckert, toujours vert!', *L'Evénement du jeudi* (21–27 July 1994), pp. 84–7

Gaulle, Charles de. *Discours et messages I* (Paris: Plon, 1970)

Golsan, Richard. *Vichy's Afterlife: History and Counterhistory in Postwar France* (Lincoln, NE: Nebraska University Press, 2001)

Gordon, Bertram M. *Collaborationism in France during the Second World War* (Ithaca, NY and London: Cornell University Press, 1980)

Gordon, Bertram M. (ed.), *Historical Dictionary of World War II France: The Occupation, Vichy and the Resistance, 1938–1946* (Westport, CT: Greenwood Press, 1998)

Gorrara, Claire. 'Cultural intersections: the American hard-boiled detective novel and early French *roman noir*', *Modern Language Review*, 98:3 (2003), 590–601

Gorrara, Claire. *The Roman Noir in Post-War French Culture: Dark Fictions* (Oxford: Oxford University Press, 2003)

Gorrara, Claire. 'Reflections on crime and punishment: memories of the Holocaust in recent French crime fiction', *Yale French Studies*, 108 (2005), 131–45

Gorrara Claire (ed.) *French Crime Fiction* (Cardiff: University of Wales Press, 2009)

Grimbert, Philippe. *Un secret* (Paris: Editions Grasset et Fasquelle, 2004)

Halbwachs, Maurice. *On Collective Memory*, edited and translated by Lewis A. Coser (London/Chicago: University of Chicago Press, 1992)

Halimi, André. *La Délation sous l'occupation* (Paris: L'Harmattan, 1983)

Hall, Katharina and Kathryn N. Jones (eds). *Constructions of Conflict: Transmitting Memories of the Past in European Historiography, Culture and Media* (Bern: Peter Lang, 2011)

Hewitt, Leah D. *Remembering the Occupation in French Film: National Identity in Postwar Europe* (Basingstoke: Palgrave Macmillan, 2008)

Higginson, Pim. *The Noir Atlantic: Chester Himes and the Birth of the Francophone African Crime Novel* (Liverpool: Liverpool University Press, 2011)

Hirschfeld, Gerhard and Patrick Marsh (eds). *Collaboration in France: Politics and Culture during the Nazi Occupation, 1940–1944* (Oxford: Berg, 1987)

Hodgkin, Katherine and Susannah Radstone (eds). *Memory, History, Nation: Contested Pasts* (New Brunswick/London: Transaction Publishers, 2007)

Hoffman, Stanley. *Decline or Renewal? France since the 1930s* (New York: Viking Press, 1974)

Hutton, Margaret-Anne. 'From christ-killers to christ-figures: representations of Jews in post–1980 French occupation fiction', *French Cultural Studies*, 18:1 (2007), 107–24

Ironside, Elizabeth. *A Good Death* (London: Hodder & Stoughton, 2000)

Jacquet, Michel. *Une occupation très romanesque: ironie et dérision dans le roman français sur l'occupation de 1945 à nos jours* (Paris: Les Editions La Bruyère, 2000)

Jardin, Alexandre. *Des gens très bien* (Paris: Bernard Grasset, 2010)

Jardin, Pascal. *La Guerre à neuf ans* (Paris: Grasset, 1971)

Judt, Tony. 'The past is another country: myth and memory in post-war Europe', in Jan-Werner Muller (ed.), *Memory and Power in Post-War Europe: Studies of the Presence of the Past* (Cambridge: Cambridge University Press, 2002), pp. 157–83

Kansteiner, Wulf. 'Finding meaning in memory: a methodological critique of collective memory', *History and Theory*, 41:2 (2001), 179–97

Kedward, Roderick. 'The maquis and the culture of the outlaw (with particular reference to the Cevennes)', in Roderick Kedward and Roger Austin (eds), *Vichy France and the Resistance: Culture and Ideology* (London: Croom Helm, 1985), pp. 232–51

Kedward, Roderick. 'Re-rooting the resistance in post-war France', in Heiko Feldner, Claire Gorrara and Kevin Passmore (eds), *The Lost Decade: the 1950s in European History, Politics, Society and Culture* (Cambridge: Cambridge Scholars Press, 2011), pp. 60–74

Kelly, Michael. 'The view of collaboration during the "après-guerre"', in Gerhard Hirschfeld and Patrick Marsh (eds), *Collaboration in France: Politics and Culture during the Nazi Occupation, 1940–1944* (Oxford: Berg, 1987), pp. 239–51

Bibliography

Kitson, Simon. 'Creating a "nation of resisters"? improving French self-image, 1944–6', in Monica Riera and Gavin Schaffer (eds), *The Lasting War: Society and Identity in Britain, France and Germany after 1945* (Basingstoke: Palgrave Macmillan, 2008), pp. 67–85

Krajenbrink, Marieke and Kate M. Quinn (eds). *Investigating Identities: Questions of Identity in Contemporary International Crime Fiction* (Amsterdam: Rodopi, 2009)

Lacan, Jacques. *Ecrits* (Paris: Editions du Seuil, 1966)

Lacassin, Francis. *Mythologies du roman policier* (Paris: UGE, 1974)

Lagrou, Pieter. *The Legacy of Nazi Occupation: Patriotic Memory and National Recovery in Western Europe, 1945–1965* (Cambridge: Cambridge University Press, 2000)

Lamberti, Elena and Vita Fortunati (eds). *Memories and Representations of War: The Case of World War One and World War Two* (Amsterdam: Rodopi, 2009)

Le Garrec, Evelyne. *La Rive allemande de ma mémoire* (Paris: Editions du Seuil, 1981)

Lloyd, Christopher. *Uranus and la tête des autres* (Glasgow: University of Glasgow French and German Publications, 1994)

Lloyd, Christopher. *Collaboration and Resistance in Occupied France: Representing Treason and Sacrifice* (Basingstoke: Palgrave/Macmillan, 2003)

Margalit, Avishia. *The Ethics of Memory* (Cambridge, MA: Harvard University Press, 2002)

Mathy, Jean-Philippe. 'Transmission problems: memory, community and the republican idea in contemporary France', *Journal of European Studies*, 35:2 (2005), 237–45 (238)

Matzke, Christine and Susanne Mühleisen (eds). *Postcolonial Postmortems: Crime Fiction from a Transcultural Perspective* (Amsterdam: Rodopi, 2006)

Maxence, Jean-Luc. *L'Ombre d'un père* (Paris: Editions Libres Hallier, 1978)

Merfeld-Langston, Audra L. 'From text to screen: portraits of collaboration in *Uranus*', *French Cultural Studies*, 21:3 (2010), 178–91

Meyhoff, Karsten Wind. 'Digging into the secrets of the past: rewriting history in the modern Scandinavian police procedural', in Andrew Nestingen and Paula Arvas (eds), *Scandinavian Crime Fiction* (Cardiff: University of Wales Press, 2011), pp. 62–76

Michel, Henri. *Histoire de la Résistance en France (1940–1944)* (Paris: Presses Universitaires de France, 1950)

Modiano, Patrick. *La Place de l'étoile* (Paris: Gallimard, 1968)

Modiano, Patrick. *La Ronde de nuit* (Paris: Gallimard, 1969)

Modiano, Patrick. *Les Boulevards de ceinture* (Paris: Gallimard, 1972)

Moeller, Robert. *War Stories: The Search for a Useable Past in the Federal Republic of Germany* (Berkeley, CA: University of California Press, 2003)

Moore, Brian. *The Statement* (London: Bloombury Publishing, 1995)

Bibliography

Morris, Alan. *Collaboration and Resistance Reviewed: Writers and the Mode Rétro in Post-Gaullist France* (Oxford: Berg, 1992)

Morris, Alan. 'From social outcasts to stars of the mainstream: the combatants of the collaboration in post-war France', *Journal of War and Culture Studies*, 2:2 (2009), 167–79

Morris-Dumoulin, Gilles. *Le Forçat de l'Underwood* (Paris: Manya, 1993)

Müller, Elfriede and Alexandre Ruoff. *Le Polar français: crime et histoire* (Paris: La Fabrique Editions, 2002)

Muller, Jan-Werner (ed.) *Memory and Power in Post-War Europe: Studies of the Presence of the Past* (Cambridge: Cambridge University Press, 2002)

Myers, Mitzi. 'Storying war: an overview', in Elizabeth Goodenough and Andrea Immel (eds), *Under Fire: Childhood in the Shadow of War* (Detroit, MI: Wayne State University Press, 2008), pp. 19–27

Nettelbeck, Colin. 'Getting the story right: narratives of the Second World War in post-1968 France', in Gerhard Hirschfeld and Patrick Marsh (eds), *Collaboration in France: Politics and Culture during the Nazi Occupation, 1940–1944* (Oxford: Berg, 1987), pp. 252–93

Nora, Pierre. 'Mi-vainqueur, mi-vaincu', in Anne Simonin and Hélène Clastres (eds), *Les Idées en France (1945–1988): une chronologie* (Paris: Gallimard-*Le Débat*, 1989), pp. 27–33

Ory, Pascal. *Les Collaborateurs 1940–1945* (Paris: Editions du Seuil, 1976)

Passerini, Luisa. 'Memories of resistance, resistances of memory', in Helmut Peitsch, Charles Burdett and Claire Gorrara (eds), *European Memories of the Second World War* (Oxford: Berghahn Books, 1999), pp. 288–96

Paxton, Robert. *Vichy France: Old Guard and New Order 1940–1944* (New York: Columbia University Press, 1972)

Pearson, Nels and Marc Singer (eds). *Detective Fiction in a Postcolonial and Transnational World* (Farnham: Ashgate, 2009)

Peitsch, Helmut. 'Studying European literary memories', in Helmut Peitsch, Charles Burdett and Claire Gorrara (eds), *European Memories of the Second World War* (Oxford: Berghahn Books, 1999), pp. xiii–xxxi

Peitsch, Helmut, Charles Burdett and Claire Gorrara (eds). *European Memories of the Second World War* (Oxford: Berghahn Books, 1999)

Perrin, Raymond. *Histoire du polar jeunesse: romans et bandes dessinées* (Paris: L'Harmattan, 2011)

Platten, David. 'Origins and beginnings: the emergence of detective fiction', in Claire Gorrara (ed.), *French Crime Fiction* (Cardiff: University of Wales Press, 2009), pp. 14–35

Platten, David. *The Pleasures of Crime: Readings in Modern French Crime Fiction* (Amsterdam: Rodopi-Chiasma, 2011)

Pons, Jean. 'Le roman noir, littérature réelle', *Les Temps modernes*, 595 (August–October 1997), 5–14

Popular Memory Group. 'Popular memory: theory, politics, method', in Richard

Bibliography

Johnson, Gregor McLennan, Bill Schwarz and David Sutton (eds), *Making Histories: Studies in History-Writing and Politics* (London: Hutchinson University Library, 1982), pp. 205–52

Quint, Michel. *Effroyables Jardins* (Paris: Editions Joëlle Losfeld, 2000)

Rigney, Ann. 'Plenitude, scarcity and the circulation of cultural memory', *Journal of European Studies*, 35:1 (2005), 11–28

Robb, Graham. *Parisians: An Adventure History of Paris* (London: Picador, 2010)

Rolls, Alistair and Deborah Walker. *French and American Noir: Dark Crossings* (Basingstoke: Palgrave Macmillan, 2010)

Rosnay, Tatiana de. *Elle s'appellait Sarah* (Paris: Librairie générale française, 2008)

Rosnay, Tatiana de. *Sarah's Key* (London: John Murray, 2006)

Rothberg, Michael. *Multidirectional Memory: Remembering the Holocaust in the Age of Decolonization* (Palo Alto, CA: Stanford University Press, 2009)

Rothberg, Michael. 'Introduction: between memory and memory, from *lieux de mémoire* to *noeuds de mémoire*', *Yale French Studies*, 118–19 (2011), 3–12

Rousso, Henry. *Le Syndrome de Vichy: de 1944 à nos jours* (Paris: Editions du Seuil, 1990)

Rousso, Henry. *La Hantise du passé (entretien avec Philippe Petit)* (Paris: Les Editions Textuels, 1998)

Sartre, Jean-Paul. 'Qu'est-ce qu'un collaborateur?', *Situations III: lendemains de guerre* (Paris: Gallimard, 1976), pp. 43–61

Stewart, Terry. *La Belle Vie* (Paris: Gallimard, 1950)

Storey, John. *Cultural Studies and the Study of Popular Culture* (Edinburgh: Edinburgh University Press, 1996)

Strinati, Dominic. *An Introduction to Theories of Popular Culture* (London: Routledge, 2004)

Suleiman, Susan Rubin. *Crises of Memory and the Second World War* (Cambridge, MA: Harvard University Press, 2006)

Suleiman, Susan. 'Memory troubles: remembering the occupation in Simone de Beauvoir's *Les Mandarins*', *French Politics, Culture and Society*, 28:2 (2010), 4–17

Todorov, Tzvetan. 'A typology of detective fiction', in *The Poetics of Prose*, trans. Richard Howard (Oxford: Blackwell, 1977), pp. 42–54

Todorov, Tzvetan. *Les Abus de la mémoire* (Paris: Arléa, 1995)

Todorov, Tzvetan. *Facing the Extreme: Moral Life in the Concentration Camps* (New York: Henry Holt, 1996)

Turnbull, Malcolm J. *Victims or Villains: Jewish Images in Classic English Detective Fiction* (Bowling Green, OH: Bowling Green University Popular Press, 1998)

Vice, Sue. *Children Writing the Holocaust* (London: Palgrave/Macmillan, 2004)

Bibliography

Virgili, Fabrice. *Shorn Women: Gender and Punishment in Liberation France* (Oxford: Berg, 2002)

Wieviorka, Annette. *Déportation et génocide: entre la mémoire et l'oubli* (Paris: Editions Plon, 1992)

Wieviorka, Annette. 'Jewish identity in the first accounts by extermination camp survivors from France', *Yale French Studies*, 85 (1994), 135–51

Wieviorka, Annette. 'From survivor to witness: voices from the Shoah', in Jay Winter and Emmanuel Sivan (eds), *War and Remembrance in the Twentieth Century* (Cambridge: Cambridge University Press, 1999), pp. 125–41

Wieviorka, Annette. '60 ans après Auschwitz: histoire et mémoire', *L'Esprit Créateur*, 65:3 (2005), 40–8

Wieviorka, Olivier. *La Mémoire désunie: le souvenir politique des années sombres de la Libération à nos jours* (Paris: Editions du Seuil, 2010)

Wolf, Joan B. *Harnessing the Holocaust: The Politics of Memory in France* (Palo Alto, CA: Stanford University Press, 2004)

Wood, Nancy. *Vectors of Memory: Legacies of Trauma in Postwar Europe* (Oxford: Berg, 1999)

Filmography

Elle s'appelait Sarah (2010, dir. Gilles Paquet-Brenner)
Hotel Terminus: The Life and Times of Klaus Barbie (1988, dir. Marcel Ophuls)
L'Armée du crime (2009, dir. Robert Guédiguian)
La Question humaine (2007, dir. Nicolas Klotz and Elisabeth Perceval)
La Rafle (2010, dir. Rose Bosch)
Lacombe Lucien (1974, dir. Louis Malle)
Le Chagrin et la pitié (1969, dir. Marcel Ophuls)
Les Hommes libres (2010, dir. Ismaël Ferroukhi)
Un secret (2007, dir. Claude Miller)

Index

Index

Index

Index

Waddington, Keir 38n.25
Walker, Deborah 38n.19
Wiesenthal, Simon 70
Wieviorka, Annette 38n.16, 44, 85
Wieviorka, Olivier 17n.2, 109
Wilkomirski, Benjamin 106–7n.38

Wolf, Joan B. 44, 55, 86
Wood, Nancy 104n.19

Yale French Studies 133

Zola, Émile 39n.25